DISCARDED

Change
Management
Excellence

D0887166

Change Management Excellence

Using the four intelligences for
successful organizational change

Sarah Cook,
Steve Macaulay,
Hilary Coldicott

**KOGAN
PAGE**

London and Sterling, VA

Publisher's note

Every possible effort has been made to ensure that the information contained in this book is accurate at the time of going to press, and the publishers and authors cannot accept responsibility for any errors or omissions, however caused. No responsibility for loss or damage occasioned to any person acting, or refraining from action, as a result of the material in this publication can be accepted by the editor, the publisher or any of the authors.

First published in Great Britain and the United States in 2004 by Kogan Page Limited

Apart from any fair dealing for the purposes of research or private study, or criticism or review, as permitted under the Copyright, Designs and Patents Act 1988, this publication may only be reproduced, stored or transmitted, in any form or by any means, with the prior permission in writing of the publishers, or in the case of reprographic reproduction in accordance with the terms and licences issued by the CLA. Enquiries concerning reproduction outside these terms should be sent to the publishers at the undermentioned addresses:

120 Pentonville Road
London N1 9JN
United Kingdom
www.kogan-page.co.uk

22883 Quicksilver Drive
Sterling VA 20166–2012
USA

© Sarah Cook, Steve Macaulay and Hilary Coldicott, 2004

The right of Sarah Cook, Steve Macaulay and Hilary Coldicott to be identified as the authors of this work has been asserted by them in accordance with the Copyright, Designs and Patents Act 1988.

ISBN 0 7494 4033 3

British Library Cataloguing-in-Publication Data

A CIP record for this book is available from the British Library.

Library of Congress Cataloging-in-Publication Data

Cook, Sarah, 1955-
  Change management excellence : using the four intelligences for successful organi-
zational change / Sarah Cook, Steve Macauley, and Hilary Coldicott.
    p. cm.
  ISBN 0-7494-4033-3
  1. Organizational change. 2. Multiple intelligences. I. Macaulay, Steve. II. Coldicott,
Hilary, 1961-III. Title.
HD58.8C6565 2004
658.4'06--dc22
                             2004009950

Typeset by Saxon Graphics Ltd, Derby
Printed and bound in Great Britain by Creative Print and Design (Wales), Ebbw Vale

Contents

Introduction

In recent years change in the business environment has become a way of life. Advancements in technology, the pace of competition, globalization, the need to control cost and increase efficiency coupled with increasing customer expectations mean that organizations have to evolve and regenerate in order to survive. Gone are the days when individuals could expect to work in the same business, under the same ownership, with the same people, and the same customer base for the whole of their career.

Management guru Charles Handy, one of the first to predict the massive downsizing of organizations and the emergence of self-employed professionals, believes that change now is a way of life. He also states something many have experienced, that 'change is always difficult'. Everyone is impacted by change.

As the degree of change increases, people who manage others, no matter what their title, are in a position to influence the process and outcomes of change. What they do and say impacts on whether others move from the comfort of the present towards a different future. Change leadership can no longer be confined to a figurehead at the top of the organization who drives change forward. In today's changing environment anyone who influences others has the capacity, through the active use of their intellects or types of intelligence, to become transformational leaders.

Traditionally, managers have kept the wheels turning. They set objectives, define procedures and monitor in order to get things done. Leaders take a more active role in change. They focus on inspiring others, setting strategies for the future, role modelling and coaching for enhanced performance. One of the key differences is the focus on the here and now as managers. The focus for leaders is on the future and looking for different ways of doing things. This is a proactive approach as opposed to a reactive one. We believe that managers must also move up to become change leaders. This view is supported by many influential management thinkers. It is outlined in Figure 0.1, which shows a model developed from the work of John Kotter. To survive in a world where the amount of change is high, and the complexity of operation is also high, businesses need people who are both strong leaders and managers.

The categories shown in Figure 0.1 can be put into context as follows:

- Considerable leadership and little management would work for a small, highly motivated group of people – perhaps doing research and development or product innovation or working for a consultancy group.

- Little leadership or management would work for a small business owner or self-employed operator, such as a window cleaner.

- Considerable management and little leadership would work in production or manufacturing where there is a lot of emphasis on managing processes or production lines and where there is little change, eg a stationery supplier getting supplies from A to B.

- Considerable leadership and management would work well in any organization where there is a large amount of change and the complexity of the operation is high, eg airlines, insurance companies, banks, the car industry, leisure industry, retail, etc.

In most organizations today, people with responsibility for others need to develop their ability to lead others towards future organizational goals. In

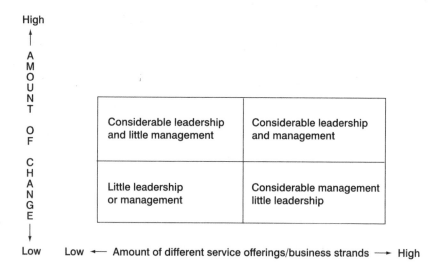

Figure 0.1 Leadership versus managership

The Flight of the Buffalo, Dr James A Belasco and Ralph C Stayer drew the analogy of the buffalo and the goose. Buffalo herds tend to follow their leader at any cost, even if doing so is injurious to the herd. Flocks of geese travel thousands of miles to their winter migration site. The geese fly in formation with the lead goose at the front of the V providing direction to the rest of the flock. During migration the geese take it in turns to lead. Each member of the flock knows the route the flock is taking and is capable of taking over the V position when the lead goose is tiring. Likewise in the business environment, managers throughout an organization need the ability to navigate the sea of change. Everyone who manages people and resources needs these skills, irrespective of their title or role.

In this book we focus on the role of leaders in intelligent change management. We take a personal view helping you to assess your own capabilities and what can be done to strengthen them.

The first chapter begins with the change leadership compass, outlining the leadership qualities needed to manage change successfully. The subsequent chapters focus on each of the four axes of the compass:

- business intelligence (BQ), which drives the context for change and provides the rationale for change;

- political intelligence (PQ), which helps leaders identify the stakeholders in change and how to influence them appropriately;

- spiritual intelligence (SQ), which provides the inner drive for change and manifests itself in the vision and values of an organization going forward;

- emotional intelligence (EQ), which supports change in oneself and others by recognizing reactions to change and creating an environment where others feel motivated to follow.

In each chapter we provide practical examples of how to navigate change and how successful leaders have applied the approaches described, as well as the opportunity for you to assess your own skills and abilities and identify where and how you can improve your capacity in order to excel at change management.

Leaders during change are like the captain of a ship. They may have a map of the seas they sail and they may know their intended destination but they must rely on their compass to navigate a pathway. They must be prepared for all eventualities: squally weather, foreign ports, truculent crew, uncharted waters and attacks by pirates. This book aims to help you navigate your way towards excellent change management so that you reach your ports of destination as quickly and effectively as possible.

1

The change leadership compass

This chapter introduces the change compass and explores the role of the leader in successfully managing change. The following points are discussed:

- What is the change compass?
- What are the leadership qualities needed to manage change successfully?
- How strong are your change management skills?
- How can you develop these qualities?

THE CHANGE COMPASS

Recent research has illustrated that the most important qualities of effective change leaders are not the disconnected set of skills or knowledge that they possess. Rather, these qualities relate to four intellects or types of intelligence: business intelligence (BQ), political intelligence (PQ) and spiritual and emotional intelligence (SQ and EQ). Depicted as four points of a compass, these intellects help leaders to navigate the stormy waters of change.

Like the four points of a compass, these intellects have equal weight. If the leader is missing one or more of them, the compass becomes unbalanced and unreliable, the pathway unclear.

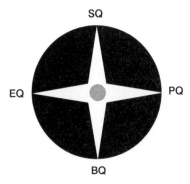

Figure 1.1 The compass of the intellects

So what are the four intellects and how does the leader use them to bring about change?

BUSINESS INTELLIGENCE (BQ)

BQ involves:

- business expertise/competence;
- thinking ahead strategically;
- listening to and anticipating customer demands;
- planning to meet customer demands;
- developing customer-driven offerings and solutions;
- taking opportunities to improve services to the customer.

Leaders with BQ anticipate changing customer demands. They translate this knowledge into service offers and operational processes that deliver successfully to the customer. They are proactive in managing customer expectations and ensure that their businesses are customer friendly.

Stelios Haji Ioannou typifies someone with high BQ. When he established his business, easyJet, he aimed to provide a low cost, no-frills style which anticipated a growing trend towards inexpensive travel. His model has challenged and changed the face of European travel. It has been extended into other areas such as car rental and the Internet where he has stripped out complicated and expensive business procedures. Although it is early days in terms of applying his model to a wide range of sectors he has made it easy for customers to do business with his organization while still opening up the possibility of making money.

EMOTIONAL INTELLIGENCE (EQ)

Emotions and feelings play a much bigger role in change than is sometimes recognized in a rationally oriented management world. The ability to recognize one's own and others' emotions and the impact that these emotions have is critical. Behaviours that demonstrate EQ include:

- understanding one's own and others' feelings;
- listening;
- being open and empathic;
- sharing feelings;
- appreciating others.

EQ can have a direct financial impact. When researchers in the United States studied the EQ of GPs, they discovered that those with the lowest level of empathy were more likely to have been sued by their patients.

EQ relates to the quality of relationships between managers, their bosses, colleagues and direct reports. A study of leaders who took part in the BT Global Challenge Round the World Yacht Race in 2001 showed that the more successful boats tended to have skippers and crews with higher levels of EQ than those who were unsuccessful in the race.

Two other components of change leadership look at the inner resources of the leader. SQ and PQ are focused more internally – SQ on the self and PQ on reading the political situation within the organization and its environment.

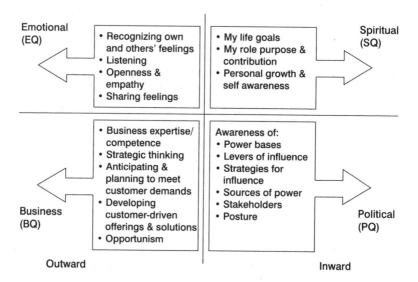

Figure 1.2 Change leadership intellects

SPIRITUAL INTELLIGENCE (SQ)

The term spiritual intelligence, or SQ, was promoted by Danah Zohar and Ian Marshall (2000) who observed that in these rapidly changing times, it was important to have a personal anchor. They described this as one's values and contribution, combined with a willingness to be receptive to new ideas and information.

Leaders with SQ display a high degree of self-confidence and self-awareness which enables them to set a clear direction and to stick firm to their course of action while not shutting out important new pieces of information. They have thought through well:

- their life and purpose;
- their role goals and contribution;
- their value to 'the world';
- how they can personally grow and develop self-awareness.

This spirituality provides inner strength and helps form a personal vision. Leaders such as Nelson Mandela and author and guru Stephen Covey display SQ through a clear set of personal values and beliefs that drive their actions. In times of change a clear sense of identity and self-belief are essential. People with strong SQ have the personal resources to drive the formulation of strong and appealing organizational visions and values that influence the behaviours of others towards future goals. Their strength of conviction gives them the confidence to think outside the box and not to be afraid to do things differently.

POLITICAL INTELLIGENCE (PQ)

In order to bring about change, leaders need to be aware of how to influence others within the organization. Every organization is political but the word also carries other negative connotations, such as self-seeking manipulation, that leads managers to shy away from its existence.

PQ as defined in this book involves:

- being aware of power bases;
- understanding sources of power;
- recognizing levers of influence during change;
- developing strategies for influence;
- gaining buy-in from stakeholders.

In the business world it is easy to be a lamb (someone who is unable to read the political situation but pleased to be part of the flock). Lambs make perfect prey for wolves – people who can read the political situation but who are out for their own end. It is best in times of change as a leader to adopt the role of the owl – wise to the political situation and focused on the good of the organization. Jack Welch, former Chairman of General Electric, is reputed to have high PQ. He led his companies through constant change and renewal, skilfully recognizing power bases and developing strategies for influence.

BQ, SQ, PQ and EQ add up to the qualities that leaders need to drive change:

- BQ provides the rationale for change, the sound business case for moving forward, the credible drive and inspiration to others.

- SQ provides the sense of purpose and the self-belief that leaders need in order to be steadfast in change.

- PQ promotes understanding of stakeholders' issues and concerns, networking and buy-in for change.

- EQ engenders positive relationships. It provides nurturing qualities and creates positive team spirit.

DEVELOPING THE INTELLECTS NEEDED TO HELP LEAD CHANGE

Unlike IQ – that many consider to be innate, mainly static in one's youth and middle years and perhaps in decline with age – the good news is that BQ, SQ, PQ and EQ can be developed whatever one's age.

It is probable, however, that people refine one or two of the intellects rather more than others and that they feel comfortable using these. In order to navigate change and to keep their boat (organization) on an even keel, effective leaders need to have high levels of intelligence in all four areas.

HOW DO YOU HANDLE CHANGE?

Using this section you can assess your change leadership style. Look at the descriptors in the four sections below. Put a tick beside the ones that you think best describe you. The results will help you to start to assess your leanings on the change leadership compass and your strengths. It is the start of a personal exploration process that will unfold as you progress through this book. In this context there are no rights and wrongs and it works best if you give your first reactions rather than to ponder for a long time over each word.

Section 1	
Quick	
Confident	
Persuasive	
Forceful	
Competitive	
Strong willed	
Inspiring	
Action oriented	
Determined	
Opinionated	
Total ticks Section 1	

Section 2	
Precise	
Deliberate	
Economical	
Analytical	
Practical	
Comfortable with details	
Questioning	
Objective	
Informative	
Authoritative	
Total ticks Section 2	

Section 3	
Trusting	
Supporting	
Responsive	
Helpful	
Receptive	
Encouraging	
Empathetic	
Sharing	
Relaxed	
Warm	
Total ticks Section 3	

Section 4	
Enthusiastic	
Creative	
Imaginative	
Persuasive	
Dynamic	
Adaptable	
Animated	
Experimental	
'Sparky'	
Inspired	
Total ticks Section 4	

Now look at the boxes with the *highest number* of ticks and the *second highest number* of ticks.

Section 1 relates to action-oriented behaviour. If your highest or second highest number of ticks is in this area your BQ and PQ is likely to be more developed than your EQ and SQ. The rationale is that your imperative for action may override concerns for individuals or perhaps block out wider, longer-term reflection and inner sense of purpose.

Section 2 relates to order-oriented behaviour. If you scored the highest or second highest in this area your PQ and BQ may be more developed than your EQ and SQ. A high score here suggests a potential rigidity in times of change, which will not easily allow new data into your mindset.

Section 3 relates to nurture-oriented behaviour. If you scored the highest or second highest in this area your EQ and SQ may be more developed than your BQ and PQ. A relatively high score implies a concern for people that can sometimes dominate the need to take objective business decisions or to take decisions to win over power bases and critical enemies.

Section 4 relates to creative-oriented behaviour. If you scored the highest or second highest in this area your SQ and EQ may be more developed than your BQ and PQ. A highly creative approach will not always settle with the realities of business and highly creative people may feel impatient with those who block fresh ideas. The highly creative may certainly be driven by their own sense of mission.

Order

PQ & BQ

These people are likely to project manage change with a clear idea of use of resources. They weigh up people and business criteria objectively. Handling known parameters is more comfortable than the unknown.

Action

BQ & PQ

A proactive, short-term focus is common with these people. They are likely to be impatient, for example if change gets blocked. They provide a strong sense of urgency.

Nurture

EQ & SQ

These people are concerned to bring others with them and strong on engaging others' support. They may be reluctant to take decisions which adversely affect others. They have a visible ethical stance.

Creativity

SQ & EQ

These people enjoy change that is new and different. They may find routine implementation dull. They have a clear, confident stance on their abilities and ideas.

Figure 1.3 Strengths and weaknesses in managing change: order, action, nurture, creativity

If you have the same score in two or three areas, look at the area/s where you have the lowest scores. These are the area/s you need to develop.

As a means of checking if your own perception of yourself is correct, ask someone who knows you well to undertake the same assessment and compare scores.

PRACTISING THE DEVELOPMENT OF POTENTIAL

We have the potential to use all points of the change leadership compass in order successfully to lead change. The first step is recognizing the need to develop each area fully. The chances are that you are well practised in using the areas at work where you scored highest. The challenge is to raise your comfort levels with the points of the compass where you scored lowest. You can do this by learning skills, attitudes and approach and then through practice, starting with easier activities and building up to harder ones.

If you find it difficult to practise the development of your potential in an organizational environment, there are activities that you can try outside work. Based on the theory of rehearsal, if you are weak in one area of intellect, you can practise activities that promote this intellect in a non-threatening environment.

Well-known people in public life have used this principle to develop their leadership qualities – for example, William Hague took up karate after becoming British leader of the opposition. His eventual failure in the role leads us to a warning: practising for development does not always guarantee success in developing all the required aspects of a role.

Below is a suggested list of activities. The chances are that if your score was low in Section 1 above (the action section) for example, you will not currently be undertaking any of the activities listed below in the action category. If your score was low for creativity, you will probably not be inclined to undertake activities in this area, and so on.

Notice your reactions to undertaking areas that are difficult for you. These reactions will give you some important clues about your reactions to change. This will be explored further later in this book.

CONCLUSION

Recent research indicates that change leaders need to be well-rounded. Our experience with many managers and organizations suggests that the qualities leaders need successfully to promote and gain acceptance for change link to the four intellects or types of intelligence BQ, SQ, PQ, EQ as follows:

- BQ: the foresight to envision the future and the drive to move the business forward.

WORK RELATED ACTIVITY

ORDER

Keep a log of how you use your time

Analyse the results

Tidy your working environment

Set out a step-by-step change plan

Investigate the use of a project management tool or software package

Start a 'To do' list with priorities

Set yourself targets

Complete the questionnaires in this book, list the implications

ACTION

Raise your energy level – take a walk when you feel 'stale'

Identify what stops you acting – take steps to overcome obstacles

At your next meeting, decide straight away, don't defer a decision. Assess the impact

Take action, don't send an e-mail deferring action

Get fitter

Outside work, take up a new interest

Observe a colleague with a bias towards action

What are they doing and how do they operate

NURTURE

Practise listening attentively

Go and see someone, customer or colleague, instead of telephoning

Take your team out to lunch as a 'thank you'

Start seeing the positives in others

Hold reward and recognition events

Ask individuals what support they need to do a better job

Look after yourself – eat well, keep healthy

CREATIVITY

Find new ways to look at old problems and solutions

Break familiar habits. For example, go to work a different way, sit with new colleagues at lunch

Read a book by a creative entrepreneur

Set up an e-mail suggestion box for your team

Look for positives

Say 'Yes, and ...' instead of 'Yes, but ...'

Do a mind map instead of a traditional report

Brainstorm opportunities for new, creative change ideas

NON-WORK RELATED ACTIVITY

ORDER

Ordering/tidying

Clearing clutter

Time management

Action planning

Reviewing

Gathering information

Strategy games

Chess/bridge

Organizing wardrobe/study

Reading

Serious classical music – Bach

ACTION

Competitive sports

Working out – gym

Martial arts – karate

Punch bag

Physical tasks/targets

Extreme sports

Rock music

NURTURE

Relaxation

Walk in nature

Bath

Proper diet

Gardening

Massage – aromatherapy

Tai chi / Yoga

Music – slow, choral, chanting

CREATIVITY

Artistic – painting

Dance class

Singing

Poetry

Pottery

Playing/self-expression

Spontaneity

Doing the unfamiliar

Jazz music

Figure 1.4 Activities to practise potential

Adapted from 'Inspirational leadership' by Richard Olivier (2001)

- SQ: knowing who you are, self-belief and sense of purpose. Creativity is a sub-set of this intelligence.

- PQ: knowing the bases of power, who to influence and how.

- EQ: recognizing feelings during change, building strong trusting relationships.

Although we have the ability to use all of these intellects, some are more developed than others. Once fully matured, they serve as a compass with which to successfully navigate change.

The chapters that follow will help you better use all four intellects. First there is a chapter on BQ which allows you to set direction and strategy for your organization to move it forward. Next comes SQ, which adds depth to the direction and strategy you wish to take. In order to encourage employees to embrace change you need to adopt the tactics of PQ. Finally, EQ will give you approaches to better understand yourself and others in order to get the best from the essential human element of the business.

This book can be read as a whole or you can use the diagnostic grid below to identify areas that you need to develop. You can then focus your attention on the chapters that deal specifically with each intellect.

ASSESSING WHERE YOU FIT ON THE CHANGE LEADERSHIP COMPASS

Assess your intellects on the scales below, by putting an 'X' on the line at the point you believe is closest to where you currently fit. Use this to help focus your attention on relevant areas of the book. Make notes in the spaces provided to remind you.

BQ

I have a good 'feel' for business issues and their implications	Most times I am aware of how my decisions are impacted by business	I don't trouble my head with wider business issues

Notes:

_____

_____

_____

SQ

I have a strong sense of my values and a wider 'sense of purpose'	On most occasions I know where I stand	I respond to circumstances – I don't worry about any purpose

Notes:

_____

_____

_____

PQ

Use of politics and power are part and parcel of my managerial task and power	When the need arises I take account of a certain amount of politics	I avoid politics at all costs

Notes:

_____

_____

_____

EQ

I take account of and I am comfortable with the level of my own and other people's feelings	When feelings are evident I normally take them into account	I am very wary and uneasy when awareness feelings come into the equation

Notes:

_____

_____

_____

2

Introduction to business intelligence (BQ)

BQ is the intelligence needed to scan the business environment and make decisions to shape the future direction of the organization. This chapter covers the following areas:

- What is BQ?
- How is BQ useful in introducing change?
- Failures in change management and how these can be avoided.

DEFINING BQ

BQ can be described as:

- business expertise and competence;
- thinking ahead strategically;
- listening to and anticipating customer demands;
- planning to meet customer demands;
- developing customer-driven offerings and solutions;
- taking opportunities to improve the organization for the future.

The food sector in the UK is a highly competitive environment that calls for strong business intelligence. When Archie Norman, ex-Chief Executive of

Asda, took over the business in 1991 he inherited a traditional Northern supermarket chain trading at a loss. His business acumen turned the company into one where strong core beliefs and a focus on value led to profitable growth and a loyal customer base. When Wal-Mart acquired Asda in 1999 CEO David Glass commented: 'I have not seen such passion for a company among its employees – except at Wal-Mart.'

Similarly, Tesco has transformed itself to become UK market leader. Tesco's skilful collection of customer data via its Club Card loyalty scheme has led it to both _anticipate_ and meet customer needs. In January 2004 Tesco's CEO, Sir Terry Leahy, was hailed the continent's best business brain by prestigious _Fortune_ magazine. Under Leahy, Tesco claims almost 27 per cent of all British supermarket sales. Leahy's success as a mass-market retailer is very much driven by the fact that he has not lost touch with his customers. His unpretentious style is in tune with Tesco's no-frills corporate culture and every year he spends a week working on the shop floor. Both Norman and Leahy show strong BQ.

USING BQ TO INFORM CHANGE

One of the certainties of organizational life is that change is constant. Change is not limited to one event, programme or initiative. In business today employees can expect an ongoing series of boundless changes rather than discrete and controlled events. As one manager in a financial services organization commented:

> In the five years that I have been with the organization not a month has gone by without some form of change occurring. Forced on us by external factors such as financial service regulations, we have also seen the change of CEO and every single one of the original senior management team have moved on. We have experienced change in technology, redundancy, relocation and restructure.

Markets, technology and products are constantly changing: customers are becoming ever more demanding, quality and service standards are constantly going up. BQ is the acumen that leaders need to scan and read the rapidly changing environment.

Fast-moving technological change, globalization and increased competition have altered the business landscape for many organizations. The Organization for Economic Cooperation and Development (OECD) estimates that manufacturing now makes up less than 20 per cent of member states' GDP. Service industries account for between a half and three-quarters of the value of member states' output.

Advances in technology, particularly the Internet, have led to changes in buying patterns and consumer demand. Organizations such as e-Bay have grown in popularity through offering the consumer the opportunity to buy and sell according to demand. Retailers such as Amazon have transformed the traditional 'bricks and mortar' approach to selling books by creating a 'virtual shopping experience'. Their online approach emulates many of the aspects of a good quality traditional bookseller by offering the buyer reviews and complementary recommendations while personalizing the transaction and making it simple and easy to do business.

Consumer desires and expectations are changing. Advertisers have coined the term 'kidult' to describe 20–35-year-olds who spend hours in front of the Sony PlayStation and break all rules of age-related marketing. Older consumers are becoming increasingly important to companies. People aged over 60 now account for 20 per cent of the UK population. It is reckoned that people over 50 control three-quarters of all assets in the UK and half of discretionary consumer spending power. Yet many consumers are time-poor. In the decade to 1996, the number of hours spent in shopping malls by the average US citizen dropped from seven hours per month to two and a half.

The increasing development of technology and loss of cross-border trade restrictions has led to the rise of globalization. The OECD reports that cross-border mergers and acquisition and strategic alliances grew more than five fold between 1990 and 2000. International joint ventures and strategic alliances increased six fold during the same period. Statistics published in November 2003 by the Office for National Statistics in UK show that the volume and value of mergers and acquisitions involving UK companies grew 14 per cent between the second and third quarter of 2003 alone. Utilities companies in the UK now have French, German and US parent companies. Rolls-Royce transformed itself into a global company because the market for aero engines was becoming international. With much of its business centered on North America it created a series of global technical centres of excellence rather than basing all the work in the UK.

A NEW WAY OF DOING BUSINESS

BQ is key in a business environment where all the rules are being rewritten. The Internet has opened new channels to market. Organizations are structuring themselves along new lines. In response to increased competition, many businesses have developed strategic alliances and partnerships to gain competitive advantage. Here organizations join together to offer 'a full service package' to customers. This is particularly helpful to businesses who have limited resources or who want to share business risk. Alliances and partnerships particularly dominate the IT world. Vendors of software and services form alliances with hardware vendors to gain a greater share of the marketplace. Increasingly firms share resources with each other to develop new products, enhance production and purchasing power and share marketing campaigns and expenditure. Such practices or 'bundled services' result in improved performance and productivity.

Computer company Dell has revolutionized the market for corporate computers. Catering for the corporate market or single user, Dell's products are bought online. Its philosophy is 'keep it simple'. Dell does not manufacture anything that can be made cheaper by another company.

The rise of the use of the Internet, increased competition and changing lifestyles has led to greater consumer demand. There is a trend towards mass customization and goods and services geared to niche markets. In the travel industry for example, short breaks and tailor-made breaks rather than packaged holidays have increased in popularity. Budget airlines such as Ryanair and easyJet now make a weekend break as affordable as a meal in a classy restaurant.

A further driver of change is deregulation. The UK car industry, for example, has seen the withdrawal of the 'block exemption' ruling. Prior to 2003 the European Union allowed manufacturers in the UK the right to select and appoint approved dealerships to sell their brand of cars. With block exemption coming to an end garages throughout the UK have the right to sell any make of car. Deregulation has also had great impact on sectors such as utilities, telecommunications and financial services in the UK.

INCREASED STAKEHOLDER DEMANDS

Business leaders need to be aware of the needs and demands of their key stakeholders more than ever before. There is a trend towards shareholders playing an increasing role in shaping the way organizations are run. When ITV companies Carlton and Granada merged, shareholders were unhappy with the appointment of Michael Grade as Chief Executive. The banks that were the major shareholders demanded his resignation and eventually a new chief executive was appointed.

In 2003 institutional shareholders were also prepared to use their voting power to veto pharmaceutical company GlaxoSmithKline's proposed senior management remuneration increases. The primary concern was that should the company underperform and the chief executive be forced to resign, there should not be contractual arrangements allowing a huge pay-off. Increasingly shareholders are becoming involved in corporate governance.

In public sector organizations, key stakeholders such as government shape strategy. The rail network has undergone a series of massive changes brought about by privatization and further transport and financial initiatives by various government departments. The National Health Service, too, has been shaped and its policies dictated by governmental and other stakeholder demands.

A further influence on change is the leadership of organizations. Shareholders are less tolerant of CEOs who in their eyes do not perform. In the world's largest companies, 10 per cent of CEOs are replaced each year. It is very rare nowadays to find CEOs such as Jack Welch, who had tenure of 20 years at General Electric. Even Welch has seen strong shareholder criticism for his continuing level of benefits and remuneration.

THE PSYCHOLOGICAL CONTRACT

Not only have pressures external to the organization increased the need to demonstrate BQ, but also internal pressures have risen.

There has been a fundamental shift in the psychological contract employees have with the organization that employs them. The term 'psychological contract' was first used in the early 1960s, but became more popular following the economic downturn in the early 1990s. In an article entitled 'Benchmark or Bandwagon' by Carol Kennedy, published in *Director* in February 2004, the term was defined as '... the perceptions of the two parties, employee and employer, of what their mutual obligations are towards each other'.

Gone are the days when an individual expected or wanted to work for the same organization for life. Charles Handy has identified that working to make a living alone is no longer all that people look for from work. 'Money becomes a crude measure of success – we are looking for something more.' He thinks of people searching to find 'uniquely what you can give to the world.' The chapters on SQ deal with this phenomenon in more depth.

Changes in the work environment include the following:

- The nature of jobs has changed: more employees are on part-time and temporary contracts, more jobs are being outsourced, tight job definitions are out, functional flexibility is in.

- Organizations have downsized and delayered: 'leanness' means doing more with less, so individual employees have to carry more responsibility.

Figure 2.1 Driving forces for change

- Technology and finance are less important as sources of competitive advantage: 'human capital' is becoming more critical to business performance in the knowledge-based economy.

- Traditional organizational structures are becoming more fluid: teams are often the basic building block, new methods of managing are required.

Younger people – the so-called 'generation X' – want excitement, a sense of community and a life outside work. They are not interested, as some of their fathers and mothers were, in a 'job for life', nor do they believe any organization can offer this to them. They expect to be treated as human beings.

A study undertaken in 2000 by Australian Financial Review found that young people were looking for a work environment very different from the current workplace. The current workplace was perceived by respondents in the survey as 'ego-centric', 'controlling' and 'authoritarian'. Young people were looking for egalitarian, team-oriented, relaxed and sociable work environments. They particularly sought organizations where 'you could be yourself' and where listening, feedback, recognition and learning were key cultural values.

USING BQ TO INTRODUCE CHANGE

BQ helps initiate and drive organizational change. When famous motorbike company Harley-Davidson faced near bankruptcy in the 1980s, the leadership team's challenge was to keep the workforce focused on creating high-quality motorbikes. Once standards had been improved the business was able to ramp up to building loyalty amongst its customer base via offerings such as the ability to customize bikes and the development of Harley Owners Groups. The latter created a sense of community and pride in the product amongst customers. Harley-Davidson also developed a series of organizational values and communication forums to engage employees. It sent production teams to visit customers to learn at first hand about the customers' needs and also sent teams to visit similar manufacturing plants to see how Harley-Davidson could be more competitive.

BQ involves:

- *anticipating* the future;

- creating *dissatisfaction* with the present;

- *mapping* a path to the future.

TYPES OF CHANGE

Organizations can be subject to incremental (morphostatic) change and step (morphogenic) change. Incremental change involves a series of minor changes over a period – or infinitely to 'fine tune' the organization (in an active sense) or to adapt reactively to market conditions. Step change occurs when an organization takes advantage of a major opportunity (reorienting itself to anticipate market demands). It can also occur when faced with a major problem and where the organization has to 'reinvent' itself to survive. Examples of reactive reinventory change include downsizing, merging or re-engineering all processes.

Part of BQ is also knowing where to focus the change and how to 'market' it. Change at organizational level is often packaged in the form of a programme, initiative or series of events aimed at moving the organization towards a stated vision or strategic aim. The advantage of such methods is that they provide a framework through which to introduce change. The disadvantage is that the change process becomes an initiative which cynics may view as 'flavour of the month'.

Here is a list of typical 'programme-led' change initiatives that you may have encountered in your working life, together with a brief description of what they involve.

Look at the following table of change programmes and tick the right-hand boxes as appropriate.		
Change programmes	Currently in place in your organization	Experienced in the past
Business process re-engineering (BPR) Redefining the processes within the organization to make them more efficient and effective		
Lean manufacturing Aimed at manufacturing organizations, the intention is to eliminate wasteful processes and make the organization more cost effective		
Six Sigma Championed by organizations such as General Electric, Six Sigma denotes a practically defect-free process (sigma is the Greek word for defect). Used by manufacturing industries and increasingly by service industries to eliminate process error		

Change programmes	Currently in place in your organization	Experienced in the past
Total quality management (TQM) A methodology again pioneered in manufacturing industries for improving the quality of organizational output		
ISO 9000 Accreditation given to organizations who can prove that they have a documented system of quality management		
Business excellence model A model of organizational excellence (also referred to as EFQM) against which businesses can benchmark themselves. Popular among public sector and private sector organizations		
Values programmes Aimed at embedding organizational values into the organization and in so doing changing the culture of a business to match the values		
Brand alignment Name given to a programme or initiative intending to align the behaviours of employees to the brand		
Service excellence/customer care Initiative to create greater customer awareness and focus on customers' needs		
Balanced scorecard Method of measuring company performance based on the following elements: – Financial – Customer – Process – Learning & Innovation		
Culture change Programme intended to change the culture of an organization		

Change programmes	Currently in place in your organization	Experienced in the past
Competency framework The introduction of a process of performance management based on competencies or skill sets		
Programmes or projects Specific programmes (a series of projects) or separate projects aimed at bringing about change, eg – Diversity – Empowerment – Introduction of SAP – Best value (public sector organizations) – Knowledge management		

List other change programmes in which you have been involved that are not covered in the above.

You will probably encounter many such initiatives in your working life. One organization with whom we work had attempted 10 of the 13 methodologies listed above in the past 10 years.

Many change programmes follow 'fads' or management trends. Typically these last two to three years. Applying the 'biblometric' method of counting the number of references in management literature, US academics found that between 1980 and 1982, 90 per cent of Fortune 500 companies had adopted 'quality circles'. By 1987, more that 80 per cent had abandoned them.

Total quality management (TQM) and business process re-engineering (BPR) were similarly charted and found to have peaked in four to six years – TQM in 1993 after launching in the late 1980s and BPR in 1995 after Hammer and Champy's much-hyped book, *Re-engineering the Corporation*, appeared in 1991.

THE RATE OF FAILURE OF CHANGE

No wonder, given the diversity of success criteria and the many levels and types of change, that all change is not successful. The failure rate of change can be high. Maurer (1997) estimates that:

- changes to do with technology have a failure rate of 20 per cent;
- changes to do with mergers and acquisitions run at 29 per cent;
- 30 per cent of changes from BPR fail;
- 50 per cent of quality improvement changes fail.

Part of BQ is knowing why so many change programmes fail and taking steps to avoid these reasons.

PITFALLS IN CHANGE MANAGEMENT AND HOW THESE CAN BE AVOIDED

Change rarely follows a bounded process no matter how much preparation you undertake. A recent study identified common reasons for failure as:

- lack of compelling reasons for change;
- unclear goals and objectives for change;
- lack of planning;
- lack of ongoing sponsorship at the highest level;
- competing projects/situations distracted attention;
- external factors having an adverse effect;
- failure to involve all those who will be affected by change;
- setting unrealistic timescales.

John Kotter, Harvard Business School Professor of Leadership, also cites the reasons why change fails – specifically managers:

- allow too much complacency;
- fail to create a sufficiently powerful guiding coalition;
- underestimate the power of vision;
- fail to create short-term wins;
- neglect to anchor changes firmly in the corporate culture.

Certainly, in our experience, embedding change into a 'business as usual' is a key component in making change work so that it is not seen as merely an 'initiative'. Change also requires a great deal of personal commitment and energy.

A CAUTIONARY WORD ABOUT BQ

The DTI published a report in 1995 ('Winning') that identified that the most successful UK companies have:

- visionary leaders who champion change;
- customer-focus teams who are empowered to make decisions;
- an ability to anticipate and respond to customer needs and expectations and constantly innovate and evolve new products and services to meet these needs.

The following chapters set out a process for enhancing your BQ in order to define a strategic direction for change. In our experience most leaders are rational and logical in their approach. In theory they can and do display BQ in their day-to-day work although they may not always operate at a strategic level. It is easy to think that having BQ alone will help initiate and influence change. However, studies show that this is not the case. Shell developed a global knowledge network that enables employees globally to turn to their international colleagues for help in solving problems. The web-based system allows engineers to share knowledge and solutions to problems. Like any change, Shell acknowledges that use of this system is about a *change of mindset* and a new way of working for many people rather than just the introduction of new technology.

We urge you to read the chapters on the other intellects that complement BQ. For example, they demonstrate the need for strong SQ during change. This allows you to hold firm in your resolve to think and question and change the rules. It provides you with the creative intelligence to drive change. In the chapter on PQ you will learn how to read the political situation and influence others. The chapter on EQ will help you relate to others and be more effective in introducing and managing change.

Change consultants Prosa have developed a change management toolkit that suggests a series of tactics that can help overcome failure during change. In order to demonstrate how BQ is complemented and enhanced by the other types of intelligence the grid below lists suggestions in relation to BQ, SQ, PQ and EQ.

Factors influencing change	BQ	SQ	PQ	EQ
Analyse the organization and its readiness for change	✓		✓	✓
Create a shared vision and common direction	✓	✓		✓
Demonstrate strong leadership	✓	✓	✓	✓
Line up political sponsorship			✓	✓
Create a sense of urgency	✓	✓		
Develop a participative implementation process			✓	✓
Communicate and involve people			✓	✓
Reinforce and recognize success		✓	✓	✓
Introduction of change	✓		✓	

3

Developing BQ

This chapter provides a framework that will help develop your BQ. This will be particularly useful for leaders who need to increase their ability to assess the business environment in which they operate and make strategic decisions about change. This chapter introduces:

- an assessment to help you rate your BQ;
- steps you can take to increase your business awareness;
- a framework for developing your BQ in relation to change.

INCREASING YOUR BUSINESS AWARENESS

Irrespective of what level you work at within the organization, BQ requires an awareness of what is happening in the macro and micro business environment that will help you initiate, plan and implement change. It also requires decision-making and planning skills.

Assess your general level of business awareness using the following simple self-assessment tool.

Statement	Yes	No
I can describe at least three of our competitors and state their competitive advantage		
I am aware of whom customers perceive as 'best in class' in our industry sector		
I can describe the economic, social, political and technological influences that affect our industry		
I am aware of future customer needs and expectations		
I can state the financial performance of my company and how this has altered over the past three years		
I can read a profit and loss statement		
I can describe the culture of my organization		
I can state the strengths and weaknesses of our organization		
I am aware of future risks facing our organization		
I am aware of opportunities that we can take in the future as an organization		
I look at a range of options before making a decision		
I make decisions in a logical fashion taking into account cause and effect		

Now count the number of 'Yes' and 'No' boxes you have ticked. If you have eight or more 'No' ticks then your BQ may need to be improved. Look over the questions again to help you assess the areas that you would like to strengthen.

STEPS YOU CAN TAKE TO INCREASE YOUR BQ

Here are some simple activities that you can undertake to increase your *general commercial awareness*:

- Read the business pages of a quality newspaper each day/week.
- Subscribe to a magazine dealing with your industry sector.

- Book yourself on to a business awareness workshop on a topic such as finance for non-financial managers.
- Look at competitors' Web sites.
- Buy competitors' products.
- Discuss the competitive environment with your manager.
- Go out with a sales person to visit customers.
- Look at the latest customer research for your organization.
- Conduct a customer survey.
- 'Mystery shop' your organization.
- Find out who operates what is considered 'best practice' in your industry.
- Attend business conferences.
- Join a local network organization.
- Gain membership of the professional body for your industry sector.

In Chapter 7 we discuss creativity and how you can generate options for the future. Here are some techniques you can use to develop your decision-making skills.

Solution matrix

A solution matrix is used to choose the most suitable solution to a problem. To do this:

- Generate possible solutions to a problem/situation that you would like to see changed.
- Decide on the criteria that are important for the solution, eg ease of implementation, impact on the problem. Two to four such criteria is probably the ideal. These criteria are written across the top of the solution matrix (see the example that follows).
- Insert a description of the problem and possible solutions in columns 1 and 2.
- Score the criteria for the solution with 1 being low and 5 being high. (Note: The scores need to be reversed if one of the criteria is 'cost'. In this case, 5 = low and 1 = high).
- Multiply the scores for each possible solution. The solution that scores the highest is most likely to be the best solution.

In this example of a solution matrix, customer service is being adversely affected within a call centre because calls are not being answered within the 10 seconds stipulated, due to the volume of calls.

Root cause	Possible solutions	Cost	Ease of implementation	Impact on problem	Acceptability to customer	Score C × E × I × A	Action Y/N
Volume of telephone calls	Employ additional staff	1	3	5	5	75	N
	Rearrange team structure	5	4	2	2	80	N
	Train staff	2	3	1	2	12	N
	Introduce voicemail service	3	5	4	1	60	N
	Internet enquiry service	2	4	5	5	200	Y

1 = Low, 5 = High.
Note: You may give weightings to each criterion if some are more important than others.

Paired-choice matrix

A paired choice matrix (see Figure 3.1) is used to reduce possible solutions to a problem. To use this matrix list all possible solutions in the left-hand column. Begin with the first row (Solution A) and proceed across the row choosing between pairs of solutions and deciding which is best. For example, there is no choice to be made between Solution A and Solution A, so you would first skip this cell and choose between Solutions A and B, writing in the box your choice between the two. Continue across the row, making a choice between Solutions A and C, A and D, and so on.

Repeat the process for each row until you have compared each possible pair. Then tally up the number of As, Bs, Cs, etc. The solution(s) that you have chosen most frequently will be your preferred one(s).

Apply one of the two decision-making techniques outlined above to a problem that you need to resolve right now.

	Solutions A	Solution B	Solution C	Solution D	Score by row
Solution A					
Solution B					
Solution C					
Solution D					

Figure 3.1 Paired-choice matrix

A BUSINESS FRAMEWORK FOR CHANGE

This section will help you increase your BQ by providing you with a business framework that you can use to initiate change.

Most leaders do not have the luxury of being in a start-up position. Richard Branson is quoted as saying: 'Our most successful companies are companies that we started from scratch'. The majority of leaders operate in well-established businesses in industry sectors that are mature or semi-mature. Whether you are operating from a start-up position or within a traditional enterprise, change begins with an evaluation of where you are now.

The three key questions that drive change management are illustrated in Figure 3.2 and this section looks at them in turn.

In the early 1990s the market for expensive sports cars declined and organizations such as Porsche were forced to take drastic action. Sales dropped by roughly a half of the peak level in the mid-1980s. The situation called for urgent action with subsequent cuts in employment numbers and production. Today Porsche has an enviable brand position and is the most profitable car manufacturer in the world. It has a three-year planning cycle that prompts its employees to assess their current position and project forward to the future.

WHERE ARE WE NOW?

BQ involves the skills of audit, analysis and decision making. The first stage in the design and initiation of change involves undertaking an objective assessment of where the organization is now in terms of strengths and weaknesses. It involves reviewing current and past performance in the eyes of customers, employees and other key stakeholders. It also involves auditing and comparing the organization to competitors and other organizations which are recognized as 'best in class'.

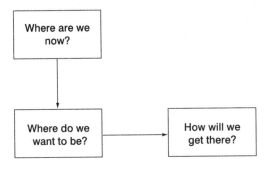

Figure 3.2 Three key questions that drive change

WHERE DO WE WANT TO BE?

This phase involves an analysis of future opportunity and the discussion of options for going forward. What do customers need and expect in the future? What are likely employee and other stakeholder demands? Once a strong vision has been created of where the organization wants to be in the future, the goals, strategy, values and behaviours of the business can be aligned to this.

HOW WILL WE GET THERE?

This phase involves the development of a strategy to achieve the objectives. It also necessitates a risk assessment and the development of a plan to move the organization forward towards the achievement of organizational goals. Considerations need to be given during this phase to the organizational underpinning, such as structure and cultural change, that may be needed to support the strategy.

TERMINOLOGY

A number of terms will be used in this and subsequent chapters to describe the components of change. These are the building blocks of change:

- vision: a picture of a desired future state that is sufficiently appealing and compelling to drive change forward;

- mission: the purpose of the organization;

- values: the underlying principles and ethics that drive the organization;

- goals: the objectives or targets that the organization is trying to achieve;

- strategy: the approach that the organization is adopting to achieve the goals that support the strategy;

- behaviours: the way in which people in the organization act in terms of what they do and say that brings the strategy and desired culture to life.

The 'corporate diamond' seen in Figure 3.3 explains the relationships between the components of change.

One company, for example, has a vision: 'to be world-class'. Its mission or purpose is: 'to satisfy customers by delivering inspirational service'. Its values are stated as follows.

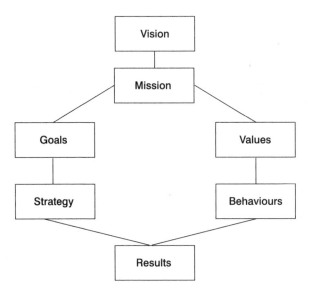

Figure 3.3 Corporate diamond

We are pioneering.

We have pace and ambition.

We have integrity.

We are hungry to learn.

Together we make a difference.

Its strategy and behaviours are aligned to its vision, mission and values.

4

Auditing the external and internal environment

This chapter provides practical guidance on techniques you can use to increase your BQ by:

- auditing the external and internal environment in which you operate;
- drawing conclusions that will help shape your future change strategy.

THE MACRO AND MICRO ENVIRONMENT

Organizations are impacted by two sets of external factors: the macro and micro environment. Sometimes called the near and the far environment, these forces for change can be summarized as shown in Figure 4.1.

PESTEL

The far or macro environment relates to the following influences (with the acronym PESTEL):

- political;
- economic;
- socio-cultural;
- technological;

Figure 4.1 The macro and micro environment

- environmental;
- legal.

These influences may impact your business, now or in the future.

Political influences relate to government or constitutional policies that may affect your business. For example, potential government legislation may allow businesses to register that they do not want to receive unsolicited calls. This may restrict cold calling on a business to business basis. To take a wider topic, the recent expansion of EU boundaries may have an impact on certain businesses.

Economic influences relate to the economy as a whole. Rates of interest have an impact, for example, on levels of borrowing. The strength of the stock market has an impact on types of investment made.

Socio-cultural influences encompass such factors as class, age and gender as well as issues such as culture and diversity. The drinking habits of people in France, for example, are different from those of people in the UK.

Technological influences include the use of the Internet, advances in mobile phones, Bluetooth and wireless networks, data management, customer relationship management systems, etc which may have an impact on your business.

Many businesses are impacted today by environmental issues. Corporate social responsibility is now higher on the public's agenda than in the past. Organizations such as Shell and Nike have been affected by adverse publicity relating to environmental issues.

Legal constraints also affect business performance. The Working Time Directive, Paternity Leave and Minimum Wage regulations are examples of this. In certain industries there are legal constraints imposed by regulatory or watchdog bodies.

The gaming industry is one sector that has been impacted by changes in the far external environment. Traditionally, betting shops such as William Hill have always been a 'horses and dogs' business. As recently as 1999 this area made up 80 per cent of its business. The proliferation of sports and topics that people can now place bets on has led to huge changes in the world of gambling. The twin forces of technology and deregulation have also altered things. Gamblers can now place bets on the Internet, via interactive TV, on WAP-enabled mobile phones, via high street shops or call centres. Bookmakers are now open on Sundays and in the evenings to cater for recent different work and leisure patterns. There are proposals on the table to modernize further the gambling laws in this country. The current laws relate back to the 1960s and license and regulate the industry.

THE NEAR ENVIRONMENT

Forces nearer to home that influence change are:

- customers;
- competitors;
- suppliers;
- other stakeholders.

Loyal customers are the lifeblood of businesses. Xerox Corporation found that loyal customers who were highly satisfied with their service were six times more likely to remain loyal to them than customers who were merely satisfied. Research by Frederick Reichheld of Bain & Company shows that a 5 per cent increase in customer loyalty equates to an increase in profitability of between 25 per cent and 80 per cent.

Customer requirements are constantly changing, as are their expectations of the quality of the service that they require. At the time of writing, the music industry has been completely revolutionized by customers' ability to download music from the Internet. Retailer Tower Records in the United States has recently filed for bankruptcy as a result of these changing consumer habits.

Business intelligent leaders spend time listening and getting close to their customers to better understand their needs and concerns, to anticipate their desires. At software company Intuit, employees followed customers who had bought their product home from the store. The objective was to understand the mindset of the customers, how they used the product and to anticipate their needs. Hotel chain Ritz Carlton set up a series of 'listening posts' throughout their hotels. Working on the basis that people closest to the customer better understood their needs and expectations, front-line managers and staff became the ears and eyes of the customer. They recorded feedback and suggestions from customers which supplemented the organization's traditional customer measurement tools, such as comments cards, surveys and 'mystery shop' visits. Airtours solicited staff views on those actions affecting customers that could be improved and how people felt about the company. This was based on the notion that the best way to develop a quality service was to enhance employees' abilities to improve the company's services. Tesco has developed a customer-oriented culture. Sir Terry Leahy, Tesco's Chief Executive, calls this 'building the business backwards from the customers' (quoted in an article entitled 'Deeper Unders' by Laura Mazur, published in *Marketing Business* in February 2004).

Just as having an understanding of the customer is a key element of BQ, leaders with high BQ have a good understanding of the competitive marketplace and ask:

- How do customers perceive our organization in comparison with competing organizations?
- What are the strengths and weaknesses of competitive organizations' products and services?
- What is each competitor's competitive advantage?
- Which organizations do customers perceive to be 'best in class'?
- How does our organization compare with these?

The Dyson vacuum cleaner has carved out a place for itself in the marketplace. Its innovative technology and design has led to a market share in the UK of approximately 50 per cent. Competitive analysis of the marketplace demonstrated that the major competitors had a poor reputation and were not perceived to be innovative or adding value.

An extension of competitor analysis is benchmarking. Benchmarking is a useful way of making comparison:

- with specific competitors;
- across an industry sector;
- with 'best in class' – although the organizations with whom you benchmark may not replicate your industry sector this is still learning to be gained.

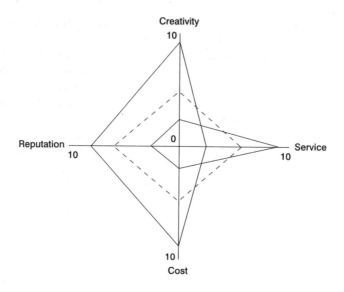

Figure 4.2 Competitor analysis for three advertising agencies

SUPPLIER ANALYSIS

The bargaining power of suppliers and the actions they take can influence your organization. In the pharmaceutical market for example while a firm has the patent for a drug and there is no comparable drug in the market-place, that firm holds considerable power.

EMERGENT OPPORTUNITIES

A review of customer, supplier and market conditions can help identify emergent opportunities. Parcelforce undertook a strategic review several years ago. It identified that there was an opportunity to target the premium end of the delivery marketplace. This in turn dictated the need for a leaner, motivated and more service-oriented organization.

INTERNAL ANALYSIS

As well as looking externally, leaders with BQ make an overall assessment of their own organization. They ask: What are we doing well? What could we do differently? Their analysis needs to cover the areas explored below.

RESOURCES

An internal audit should assess the resources of the organization in terms of finances, reputation and stakeholder satisfaction. Investors today are becoming increasingly conscious of the power of the brand. Organizations such as Coca-Cola and Orange have added significant values to their bottom line by creating powerful, global brands. A survey from the Association of Assurance and Risk Managers of the top 250 companies in the UK said damage to reputation was the biggest risk that business faced. Other bodies estimate that goodwill – of which reputation plays a key part – accounts for 70 per cent of the total value of an organization.

A financial review is imperative in assessing the organization's performance. Kaplan and Norton developed the Balanced Scorecard which provides the organization with a 'dashboard' of measures to steer the business linking to financial measures, customer measures, process measures and learning/continuous improvement.

Likewise it is helpful to review the physical resources of the organization. This will include the most powerful asset of the organization – its people. In a service environment, employees have a pivotal role to play in making or breaking reputation.

CULTURE AUDIT

Turning to the organization as a whole, frequently little may be documented on its culture. To get a wider picture of the organization and its component parts we have found a big benefit in assessing the culture of the organization. Management psychologist Schein describes culture as a phenomenon that surrounds us all. In order to understand an organization the business intelligent leader needs to understand its culture. Culture according to Schein is 'a pattern of shared basic assumptions that a group learns as it solves problems'.

It can be seen through:

- behaviour: language, customs, traditions;
- group norms: standards and values;

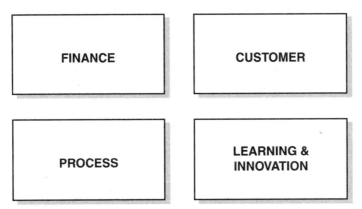

Figure 4.3 A balanced scorecard

- espoused values: published, publicly announced values;
- formal philosophy: mission;
- 'rules of the game': rules applying to all in organizations;
- climate: climate of the group in interaction;
- embedded skills;
- habits of thinking, acting, paradigms: shared knowledge for socialization;
- shared meanings of the group;
- metaphors or symbols.

One way to understand culture is to use an analytical framework. Johnson and Scholes (1993) call their framework the culture web, a series of overlapping aspects of culture which make up the collective mindset. The culture web is best considered individually and then discussed with groups of managers. For example, look at your own organization in relation to the following:

- symbols – logos, offices, cars;
- power – who has power;
- organizational structure – formal and informal structures;
- controls – what gets measured and rewarded;
- rituals – what are accepted procedures and rituals;
- stories – sometimes called 'war stories'.

A number of useful questionnaires can be used to audit your company's culture. They help to form a map of the context in which you are operating. If you do not understand and manage culture, it will manage you.

The Seven Ss diagnostic framework, developed by management consultants McKinsey, provides a useful perspective with which to assess the culture and effectiveness of an organization. The Seven Ss are:

- 1. Structure.
- 2. Strategy.
- 3. Shared values.
- 4. Style.
- 5. Staff.
- 6. Skills.
- 7. Systems.

1. Structure

There are many permutations of structure that an organization can adopt:

- centralized;
- decentralized;
- hierarchical;
- flat;
- team based;
- virtual.

Each has its pros and cons. For example, many layers of hierarchy can block a leader's access to customers and vice versa. Middle managers may 'filter' reality and present leaders with the picture of customer satisfaction that they wish them to see. The result of this is not only leaders who lack customer focus, but also employees who are fearful of 'stepping out of line' or taking responsibility for the customer.

On staying several nights recently in a well-known hotel chain, one of the authors returned to her room at 7 pm to discover that it had not been made up. With the maid waiting beside her, the guest had to speak to both the front of house manager and the housekeeping manager before eventually she was asked to pass on their permission to the maid to clean the room.

2. Strategy

The strategy of an organization shapes its structure. Likewise the behaviours and values of an organization can promote or undermine its strategy. For example, one retail business was trying to increase its customer satisfaction ratings. Although outwardly it promoted openness and responsibility, in practice managers throughout the organization were highly autocratic, secretive and reluctant to delegate. Little wonder that when the CEO announced that in an effort to be customer focused, all employees were to be empowered, no one was prepared to take up the challenge. It takes a lot of honesty and tenacity for senior managers to recognize the real values of the organization and to tackle any negatives.

Compare most businesses in many market sectors: retail, finance, leisure and airlines for example, and the majority have produced a mission statement that says they are customer focused. This is often an empty 'me too' gesture because it is not translated into actions.

In the UK at Cranfield School of Management, a program has been devised called 'Implementing Service Strategy'. It has attracted senior delegates from a very wide range of organizations. Program Director Graham Clark stresses: 'Fine words alone in a customer strategy are just empty. We help senior managers put together action plans to firm up exactly what needs to be different. We emphasize the leader's role in culture change and monitoring and measuring service performance. What senior managers do is critical.'

3. Shared values

If you discover the passion of the CEO, you will discover the organization's real priorities. Is the CEO's fundamental passion towards:

- making money;
- staff relationships;
- customer orientation?

These are important issues to get to the bottom of. What measures are used in reward systems? This often shows the reality of what is important to the organization.

Federal Express has developed nine Service Quality Indicators, all tied to customer expectations. Staff bonuses are linked to the overall performance of these indicators. This promotes an all-round customer culture.

Senior managers should be part of this process too, not just given a blanket bonus for profitability. Also, sound systems need to be set up to ensure that top managers are involved first hand in customer feedback. In the UK financial service organization, Barclays Bank, for example, bases its rewards to managers on comprehensive feedback from colleagues, staff and customers.

4. Style

How leaders behave influences the behaviours of their staff. The most effective leaders are those who are sensitive to people's needs. When senior managers' career paths have been via specialist or technical functions, for example, they may well fail to appreciate the need for a holistic approach to change. Typically where this style prevails, quantitative measures are set for operational delivery. Little attention is paid to the qualitative aspects of service such as creating rapport and being empathetic to the customer.

Senior managers are often preoccupied with other influences such as competitors, shareholders, the City, government and regulatory bodies. Customers compete against these other preoccupations for their share of airtime and often lose.

Senior managers can all too easily become cocooned in a world far removed from the customer and the company people who work at the sharp end. One acid test of how removed your senior people may be from customers is: Who replies when a customer writes to the CEO?

This remoteness frequently leads managers to:

- become hooked into the internal politics of the organization;
- shut off from honest feedback;
- rarely see the customer face to face.

This can all add up to management decisions which are far from customer-friendly, such as rules and regulations that work well for the organization but not the customer.

The new style of leadership that appears most effective in a service environment has become known as 'servant–leadership'. Here leaders have a genuine desire to serve the customer. They become actively involved in promoting excellent service through their interactions both with employees and customers themselves. Herb Kelleher at Southwest Airlines and Carl Sewell at Sewell Village Cadillac are examples of leaders with a genuine customer obsession that has enlivened and enriched their businesses.

A good example of paying attention to employees' needs with the customer in mind is financial services group First Direct. It could have followed the call-centre norm and treated employees as dispensable fodder. Instead, it consciously created a mission of a 'great place to work' and carefully thought about the needs of its employees. Since 80 per cent are women, often working in a 24-hour environment, it paid extra attention to their needs for personal security, for example with controlled parking spaces and also a large crèche facility. To give employees and customers the best possible experience, new employees are given a thorough five-week induction, accredited training, and rewards for successful performance. Managers carry out twice-yearly opinion surveys among employees – and act on the results.

First Direct has a well thought out retention strategy, involving:

- recruitment – selecting the right people who will give the customer the right experience and who are likely to stay;
- resource deployment – so that the employee is not overstretched and can deliver to the customer;
- competency definition – clarity of role;
- development using accreditations – sound development with motivational stages;
- benchmarking – to pinpoint success;
- performance management – spotting issues early and managing progress supportively;
- career management – nurturing of talent;
- reward and recognition – encouraging the right things.

Underpinning all of this is clear leadership, with pervading customer and employee-oriented values.

BUPA is another organization that knows that the success of its increased customer-focused efforts rest on careful attention to its employees. In the words of one senior manager: 'Pursuing the goal of improving staff satisfaction, loyalty and commitment was not just a liberal "good employer thing to do". It had real, tangible results for our customers and for BUPA's profitability.'

5. Staff

We are increasingly engaged within organizations to move front-line employees from a dependent, compliant and rule-bound style towards one where they freely take risks and confidently exercise discretion. The answer frequently starts with the very senior managers who bemoan the lack of initiative in their staff. People working for 'task-master' style managers who are directive and autocratic develop into terrorists – who are reluctant or resistant to change, or spectators – who take a back seat when it comes to resolving a customer problem. This is because people often become resentful or discouraged to take initiative when they are constantly told what to do and when the only feedback they receive is negative.

Organizations such as the restaurant chain TGI Friday operate rigorous recruitment policies to ensure that their people exude customer focus. They also recognize the power of management by example through active coaching and role modelling. New recruits soak up culture like sponges: they may have been recruited for their winning qualities, but they are influenced strongly by others' behaviours.

6. Skills

Customer-oriented organizations such as the department store Nordstrom in the United States emphasize the attitude and interpersonal skills needed to interact effectively with customers. Role, skills and knowledge can be taught, whereas many of the less tangible, empathetic interpersonal skills involve being able to create vital rapport with customers. Nordstrom recruit only self-starters – a high commission system helps deselect others. Each of Nordstrom's 35,000 staff effectively runs his or her own business (within limited rules).

7. Systems

The systems that organizations use to interact with their customers need to be designed with the customer in mind. The authors were reminded of this when travelling recently overseas. They used an airline which advertised: 'electronic ticketing – no documents needed'. Having duly turned up at departure without a ticket, they were told that they could not check in until they produced one!

Here is an example of part of one internal audit undertaken by leaders of an organization that wanted to assess its customer orientation:

Honestly rate customer contact against the following other priorities: financial; shareholders; regulatory external; internal stakeholders. How would you rank these five priorities, in order?

1.

2.

3.

4.

5.

When did you last speak to a customer?

Did you implement what you learnt?

How do you know what problems your people encounter when dealing with customers?

When did you last update this knowledge?

What is the gap between your organization's intended service strategy and how you really deal with the customer?

Have you reviewed your organizational structure specifically for its customer orientation?

Where do customer-facing employees sit in the hierarchy?

What messages does your leadership style send to the customer and the rest of the organization?

What feedback have you had to support this?

How do you support and strengthen your staff's abilities to deal successfully with customers?

Are your skills in giving and receiving feedback up to scratch?

Do you use them regularly?

Are you willing to tackle your colleagues about difficult issues that impede customer service?

Are the systems you operate likely to encourage customer satisfaction?

Are reward and motivation systems linked up correctly with encouraging customer satisfaction?

THINGS TO DO

- Undertake a PESTEL analysis of the far environment.

- Speak to a customer.

- Review or undertake customer research.

- Hold a customer focus group.

- 'Mystery shop' your organization and a competitor organization.

- Ask customers what you can learn from your competitors.

- Undertake a supplier audit.

- Take part in a benchmarking study.

- Analyse the financial results of your business, look also at customer, employee, process and improvement measures.

- Undertake an internal audit of your organization's culture – employee surveys are a useful measure of this.

5

Strategic analysis

This chapter focuses on:

- methods for analysing the results of the external and internal audit;
- how to generate strategic options for change.

SWOT ANALYSIS

Traditionally in organizations, not much attention has been given to understanding the true nature of the current situation, yet we believe it is vital to the success of change. Dashing headlong without careful analysis will surely lead to disappointing results. Serious consideration of such factors as competitor analysis, context, capability, motivation and culture is needed. Having gathered information about the current state this needs to be presented in a way that is clear and easy to understand.

A SWOT analysis is a helpful tool to summarize the results of an internal and external audit. SWOT stands for strengths, weaknesses, opportunities and threats. Strengths and weaknesses are internal to the organization and can be used to capture a summary of the internal audit that you have undertaken. Opportunities and threats relate to the external environment (macro and micro). Figure 5.1 shows a SWOT analysis for a GP's surgery.

A further useful analysis is to assess the organization's portfolio of products and services. The Boston Consulting Group's product/service analysis matrix (see Figure 5.2) can be useful in positioning products and services in

STRENGTHS	WEAKNESSES
Committed and long-serving staff Dedicated doctors Open management style Regular meetings New appointment system	Inability to recruit another full-time partner Premises in need of refurbishment Some people are reluctant to change Lack of development for staff

OPPORTUNITIES	THREATS
Work closer with Social Services Clinical governance means everyone has to have a development plan Funding from Trust to improve premises Greater collaboration across surgeries	Increasing list size versus number of doctors Reluctance of newly trained doctors to enter general practice

Figure 5.1 SWOT analysis

relation to their life cycle. This helps identify which products and services are most profitable and where there is potential market growth.

The matrix suggests that 'cash cows' should be milked for their cash flow and no further investment be made here. Little effort or resources should be devoted to 'dogs'. 'Question marks' can become 'stars' if investment is made in them. 'Stars' are products and services that can become more profitable and investment should be made to strengthen their relative market share.

DEVELOPING A VISION OF THE FUTURE

Once the change leader has carefully assessed where the organization is now, he or she can make informed choices about where he or she wants it to be in the future. Developing a vision of a compelling future state is an essential step in taking people with you during change.

An attractive vision of the future helps create dissatisfaction with the current state. In Chapter 12 we discuss a process for creating an organizational vision. Chapter 10 also describes how to create your own personal vision, which will help you as a leader during change.

Having a vision for your company is stretching the organization beyond its grasp. Bill Gates' vision for Microsoft is of a computer in every home. Powerful visions are compelling and memorable over time. The Carphone Warehouse, Europe's leading independent mobile communications retailer,

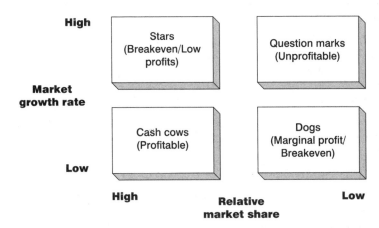

Figure 5.2 Product/service analysis

prides itself on offering customers impartial and expert advice, the widest choice of the latest product and unbeatable service. In addition to the UK, where The Carphone Warehouse has over 22 per cent market share, the company operates across 10 further European markets including Belgium, the Czech Republic, France, Germany, Ireland, the Netherlands, Portugal, Spain, Sweden and Switzerland. Outside the UK and Ireland the company operates under the brand name The Phone House. The company employs 7,500 people in total, working across the stores, support centres, call centres, online teams and direct sales teams (telesales).

The vision and core values first introduced by the company's founder, Charles Dunstone, remain unchanged since its foundation. The company continues to be driven by a dedication to customer satisfaction that has remained unswerving in spite of the many changes the organization has seen.

IDENTIFYING LONG-TERM GOALS

Once a vision has been developed, the executive team is able to create long-term goals to move the organization towards the attainment of the vision. These will be specific to each organization, but following the principles of the balanced scorecard, mentioned in Chapter 4, will generally focus on:

- increasing customer satisfaction and retention;
- improving employee satisfaction and retention;
- process improvement/operational efficiency;
- financial success.

Once the goals have been agreed, measures of success can be developed for each goal. The organizational objectives can then be cascaded into departmental and personal objectives so that each person in the business is connected to its goals and vision. One of the key steps that Lou Gestner of IBM took in turning the fortunes of the organization was to align the reward system to the attainment of organizational goals. The founder of computer giant Dell, Michael Dell (1999) states: 'You need to engender a sense of personal investment in all your employees – which comes down to three things: responsibility, accountability and shared success ... Mobilise your people around a common goal. Help them feel part of something genuine, special and important, and you'll inspire real passion and loyalty.'

VALUES AND BEHAVIOURS

The vision and goals of the organization can be supported and underpinned by the development of values and codes of behaviours that support the vision. Chapters 10 to 12 describe in more detail why this is important and also provide a framework for developing organizational values and supporting behaviours.

DEVELOPING STRATEGIES TO ACHIEVE GOALS

Having established the vision, values and goals of the organization, together with measures of success, the change leader and his or her team need to develop a strategy for achieving these. There are various options that lead to differentiation in the market place and hence competitive advantage.

These can generally be broken down into cost and other differentiators such as service, reliability and relationships. Enterprise, the car hire company that has become the biggest in the United States, outshining both Hertz and Avis, has had consistent growth rates of 20 per cent a year. The firm operates from non-airport locations and does not have the advertising revenue of its rivals. Its key differentiators are cost – its prices are as much as 20 per cent lower than typical airport rates – and service.

Business academic Michael Porter (1985) has developed a model of differentiation as follows: differentiation through distinguishing efficiencies and effectiveness derived from cost by knowing what is important to the customer and driving cost downwards; and differentiation via finding and consistently delivering products and services in ways that derive competitive advantage. A business can also have a generic focus – targeting a wide number of consumers or a specific focus – targeting a narrow spectrum of consumers.

Using these principles there are four strategic options that a business can adopt (see Figure 5.4):

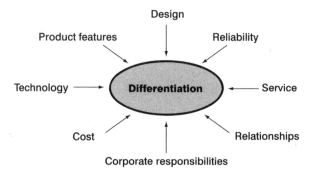

Figure 5.3 Sources of differentiation

- generic cost focus;
- targeted cost focus;
- generic differentiation focus;
- targeted differentiation focus.

In the UK supermarket sector, for example, this model of differentiation might be represented as:

Generic cost focus = Asda
Targeted cost focus = Aldi
Generic differentiation focus = Tesco
Targeted differentiation focus = Waitrose

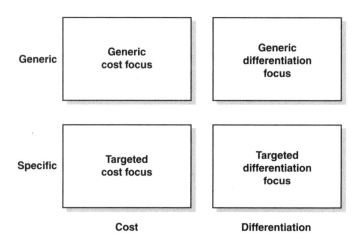

Figure 5.4 Strategic options

PROFITABLE GROWTH

In the private sector, the aim of the majority of businesses is to increase profit and growth. Ansoff (1987) describes four possible strategic options that businesses can adopt towards profit and growth, as shown in Figure 5.5.

Market penetration is where an organization develops its market share by selling a greater number of products to customers in the existing marketplace. Supermarket chain Tesco, for example, have increased their market share so that they top the supermarket league. They estimate that one pound out of every eight spent on food goes to their stores.

Market development is where a business introduces its current products and services to a new market. Tesco, for example, introduced Tesco Metro to inner-city locations thus developing a new marketplace for convenience shopping. Tesco also have developed a range of upmarket foods called 'Tesco's Finest'. This is an example of product development; offering new products/services to the existing marketplace. They have also introduced a financial service offer which brings new products/services to new marketplaces.

A further strategic option is vertical integration. This is where businesses buy suppliers so that there is a continuous loop between the consumer and the business. The travel organization TUI owns Lunn Poly travel agencies; it also owns Thompson Holidays and Britannia Airways.

SCENARIO PLANNING – WHAT IF?

The change leader needs the ability to generate strategic options. Part of this process is the ability to anticipate and think through how different options

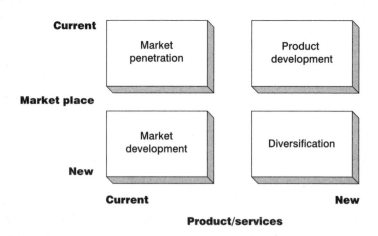

Figure 5.5 Different options

will impact the business in the future. Risk assessment and scenario planning can help you develop this process. Here groups of managers meet to develop 'What if' scenarios that help them analyse and make informed decisions about strategic options. There are risks associated with each change option. Risks are potential problems that can occur in introducing and managing change. Chapter 6 covers a process for risk assessment.

STRUCTURE

The strategy that a business adopts also informs its structure. Enterprise car rental in the United States, for example, operate each branch as a separate business/profit centre. This system fits well with its strategy of lower pricing and superior customer service as it motivates managers to perform.

One way of overcoming problems of inadequate resources or high risk is to form strategic alliances or partnerships. Increasingly many managers are facing up to some key decisions about how they resource their customer services. This often requires questions on outsourcing, for example:

- Should I outsource my customer-related activities?
- What impact will it have on the customer?
- Can we achieve better service?
- Will outsourcing save me money?
- Can the outsourcer provide a better service?
- Can I afford necessary technology advances for call centres and e-commerce?
- Can I take the risk on behalf of my customers that it might all go sour?

Outsourcing is another strategic option that is increasing in popularity. A major research study of current and future practices in outsourcing has been carried out by Cranfield School of Management. Analysis revealed that basic services such as cleaning, catering and printing were the most frequently outsourced, with HR, IT and telecommunications also often mentioned. Next in frequency of outsourcing was a middle-band response which included facilities management, e-commerce and call centres, logistics, finance/accounting and manufacturing. Least likely to be outsourced were:

- information and knowledge management;
- purchasing;
- fund management/securities/asset management.

Some organizations, such as Amazon, outsource to specialist suppliers much of their contact with the customer, for example call-centre and logistics management, and this has been a resounding success. Other businesses, such as Dell and Wal-Mart, have shown that competitive advantage can be gained by outsourcing key activities such as manufacturing and logistics. British Airways has outsourced its service and complaint handling to India.

GETTING THERE

Once strategic options have been generated and assessed, the change leader needs to measure the size of the gap that is present between desired and current states. He or she also needs to be clear on what the organization needs to stop, start and continue doing in order to implement change. This may involve aligning all organizational processes so that they support the change.

The Civil Service is facing a major change in meeting the needs of its key stakeholders: government, customers and employees. The Department for Work and Pensions (responsible for Jobcentre Plus, the Child Support Agency, the Pension Service and the Disability and Carers Service) has recognized the changing expectations of staff and customers and the need to ensure in terms of people management that its HR and other practices are aligned to this need. It has set out its vision under the overall purpose 'To promote opportunity and independence for all through modern, customer-focused services.'

Communicating vision, values, goals and strategy is a fundamental necessity to start the change programme. In the next chapter we look at best practice in planning change.

6

Implementing change

'Words are words, promises are promises but only performance is reality.'

Harold Geneen of ITT

This chapter discusses implementation and project management techniques that will help you increase your BQ in the areas of:

- planning for change implementation;
- risk assessment;
- effectively project managing the change process.

PLANNING FOR CHANGE IMPLEMENTATION

When Lou Gerstner took over the reins as the new CEO of an ailing IBM, he is quoted as saying that it was not a vision that the company needed but a focus on delivery. One of the first business judgments that he made was to reduce the price of servers as his market analysis told him that these were overpriced. He then vigorously pressed for sales implementation, reorganizing the processes to capitalize on IBM's business strengths.

Part of BQ is being able to put processes in place to ensure effective delivery of change. This is very much dependent on the buy-in of others. In Chapters 15 and 16 we talk about mobilizing and influencing others to want to change (in terms of EQ and PQ). In this chapter we focus on the phases of change management and project management techniques that are useful during change.

Larry Bossidy left General Electric to become CEO of the struggling business Allied Signal. In turning the company around, he says that the most important activity was attention to getting things done. He reckons that the way to make this happen is to focus on the people issues and he spent 40 per cent of his time doing this when he first joined the company.

Managing change can be described as consisting of four phases:

- set up;
- kick off;
- delivery;
- review.

Here is a checklist of some key aspects of what needs to happen to deliver results in each phase.

Set up

This is the planning and preparation for change. Before the change, whenever possible:

1. Prepare people for change
   Let them know what is happening in good time but not so far ahead that they forget about the change or become unduly concerned. One organization we know told their UK workforce about a planned move to Ireland ten months before the move and then gave them the details three months before the move. As a consequence there was a great deal of unrest, motivation dropped and many good employees found alternative employment before the detailed description of transfer options was announced three months before the move date.

2. Involve those affected by the change in planning for the change
   Spell out how you see the change affecting individuals and employees as a whole. Identify who will be most affected and approach them first. Involve them in planning for the change. Discuss each stage of the way and ask for suggestions.

3. Assess the organization's readiness for change.
   Research what happened during the last change. Learn from past experience and let this influence your current actions. Are people ready to undertake change? What can you do to increase their readiness for change and create dissatisfaction with the current state?

4. Make contingency plans
   Think of the reactions the proposed change could bring about. Anticipate the unforeseen, the unexpected and any setbacks. Build contingency plans.

5. Anticipate the skills and knowledge that will be needed to master the change.
   Do your staff possess these skills and knowledge? Have you prepared plans for training?

6. Set a timetable and objectives so that you can measure your progress.

Kick off

When change begins you may need to:

1. Create a project management group to oversee the change.
   Make sure that its members represent the key stakeholders during change and that their views are taken into account.

2. Develop temporary policies and procedures during the change.
   Demonstrate flexibility in trying new things. Loosen control and relax normal procedures.

3. Create new channels of communication.
   Remind people why the change makes sense. Use e-mail, newsletters, videotapes, general meetings, training sessions, posters, etc so that people will receive information fast. The cost of gossip and rumour is high; forestall it through clear, accurate information. One CEO we work with took the opportunity during change to get 'back to the floor'. He tabled three sessions each week in his diary where he walked the floor and visited branch locations simply to ask people what they were feeling and what they saw as the key issues to address. In this way he kept a finger on the pulse of change.

4. Arrange frequent meetings.
   Meet frequently to monitor the unforeseen, to provide feedback, or to check on what is happening. Make feedback a daily event.

Delivery

1. Train and coach others.
   Provide appropriate training in new skills and develop new attitudes and behaviour patterns.

2. Make people responsible.
   Inform each person that he or she is accountable for some aspect of the change.

3. Provide feedback.
   Provide more feedback than usual to ensure that people always know where they stand.

4. Allow for a drop in performance.
    People take time to adapt to new ways and initially it is fair to expect a drop in performance

5. Expect resistance.
    Do not dismiss as irretrievable people who resist change. Help people let go of the 'old'. Be ready to help those who find it particularly difficult to make the adjustment.

6. Monitor progress.
    Give people a chance to step back and look at what is going on. Ask for feedback on what is working well and what could be better. Encourage people to think and act creatively. Listen and act on employee suggestions.

Review

1. Review learning points.
    Review what has gone well and things you would do differently next time. Capture this learning for future projects.

2. Recognize those who have made special effort during change.

3. Celebrate.
    Organize special events to acknowledge publicly those groups and individuals who have helped to make things happen.

Over the past five years, the charity Guide Dogs for the Blind has successfully metamorphosed from a bureaucratic institution focused solely on training and provision of guide dogs into a modern and efficient disability charity helping improve mobility for blind and partially sighted people across the UK. The key to its success has been well-structured communication and development processes, encouraging staff to inject some 'oomph' as the charity develops new areas, including training and rehabilitation programmes.

When Geraldine Peacock was drafted in as Chief Executive to initiate this transformation in 1997, she found the staff and working culture in very poor shape. The organization was in financial free-fall, and its 950 staff and 100,000 volunteers were reeling from accusations in the national press that the charity was sitting on huge reserves of public money. An atmosphere of mistrust permeated the whole organization.

Peacock recalls the challenge that she faced: 'I knew immediately that if we were going to turn the charity round we would have to push through a culture change from within,' she explains. 'I walked into a risk-averse organization that wasn't comfortable or familiar with having an open and transparent relationship with its staff and where internal communications consisted of senior managers issuing orders and everyone jumping to.'

As a result, a high profile and extensive programme of training and personal development was launched. Backed up by the changes in its overall structure, this has helped foster the feeling that the charity is investing time and money in developing leaders in-house. Peacock adds: 'We've tried to be as transparent as possible through a series of briefing publications. These laid out a new vision for the charity by explaining the challenges faced, and the possible routes for change.'

Guide Dogs for the Blind started running a series of video briefings at every staff, trainer and volunteer centre, featuring Peacock delivering a single defined corporate message of communicating a certain aim that the charity was working towards. 'A definite "us against them" culture had developed in the regions and we needed to reach a situation where you could trust the middle manager to deliver the right messages, rather than side with the staff against the directors.'

By launching a strong and effective system of staff representation, the charity also showed staff that their views were crucial to the charity's future. (Source: an article entitled 'Leadership Unleashed' by Laura Mazur, published in _Marketing Business_ in February 2004).

PROJECT MANAGING CHANGE

Many organizations are using programme and project management techniques to implement change. In the mid-1990s, British Airways Engineering was radically reorganized through BPR. A carefully structured project approach was adopted, with hundreds of key managers and specialists involved. Unusually the same project approach was applied to the introduction of HR and cultural change.

When managing a change project or programme in this way, the project is likely to have key phases with sub-project tasks.

Set up

During the set-up phase of the project an initial scope is agreed. A feasibility study may also be undertaken for larger projects or programmes. In this phase the sponsor for the change (who is preferably at the senior leadership level) and the project manager will agree and appoint team members.

The sponsor has ultimate responsibility for the delivery of the project and should ensure that the project is value for money and is delivered within the specified timescales. He or she has ultimate responsibility for the effective management of risks and issues. He or she champions the project within the business and ensures that the change initiative brings benefits.

The project manager has the authority and responsibility to run a project on a day-to-day basis to deliver the required deliverables on behalf of the sponsor. He or she is responsible for producing the required deliverables, to the required standard of quality and within the specified constraints of time and cost. The project manager must operate within the constraints agreed by the sponsor.

Checklist for the role of project manager
Sets and agrees clear goals
Produces schedules
Establishes budgets
Estimates resources
Analyses risks and makes contingencies
Communicates the vision
Structures the team, establishes roles
Identifies individual and team needs
Agrees clear responsibilities and accountabilities
Leads and manages meetings effectively
Creates an open climate (of support and challenge)
Confronts and resolves issues
Monitors progress and holds regular reviews
Reviews individual and team performance
Recognizes and rewards effective contribution
Coaches where appropriate
Gives and seeks feedback
Listens and responds
Demonstrates effective influencing and negotiation skills
Works across boundaries
Communicates effectively to all involved
Transfers the learning
Champions and defends the team

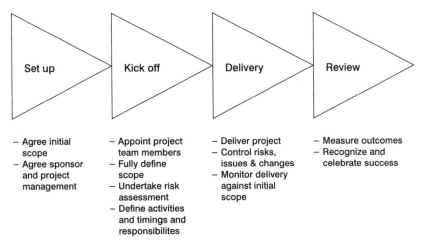

Figure 6.1 Phases of project management

Kick off

During this phase the project team is formed. Led by the project manager the first task of the team is to agree the detailed scope of the project. Here is an example of a scope document. The scope is agreed and signed off by the sponsor.

Project scoping process

Background
Justification for the project – what is this based on and what would the perceived benefits be? Who are the customers/stakeholders in the project?

Objectives

What do you want the project to achieve in SMART terms?
Which key issues will the project address/resolve?
How does the project fit in with your strategic aims?

Within scope

What are the boundaries/parameters of this project? Where do the boundaries/parameters cross with other projects?

Outside scope

What are you not looking at/including in this project?

Anticipated phases

What are the different phases of delivery?

Assumptions

What assumptions are you making about this project? (eg we have this project team as a resource for the length of the project)

Constraints
What are the constraints of this project? (eg budgetary constraints)

Timescale
Estimate timescales for each phase.

Deliverables
What are the deliverables/outputs for this project?

Estimated effort
How many people will be needed to implement the project and for how long?

Contacts
Who is the project manager and the project sponsor and what are their contact details?

Who are the project team members and what are their contact details?

Authorizations
Who has the authority to make decisions and sign off the project? (eg the project sponsor)

During the kick-off phase and throughout the delivery phase the project team will be identifying and monitoring risk. Risk management focuses attention on the chance of an event occurring that may threaten the successful delivery of a project and identifies actions (risk response) that could be taken to minimize the threat and impact of the risk.

A risk can be defined as a potential problem that may have a negative impact on the progress, costs or benefits of a project if it were to happen. Action should normally be taken to minimize or reduce the impact or likelihood of the risk, the risk response strategy could be to avoid, minimize, mitigate, transfer or accept the risk.

A risk left unattended may potentially become an issue. This is something that has happened and is causing a problem. Actions are required to avoid or decrease the impact of the problem. If action is not taken to resolve the issue this may result in changes to the scope of the project in terms of time, cost or resources.

For each risk the potential impact and likelihood is evaluated. Figure 6.2 shows the assessment criteria used by one organization in the financial services sector.

Once the impact and likelihood have been evaluated, these elements are plotted on a risk matrix (as shown in Figure 6.3) to determine their relative

Impact (of the risk materializing)	Likelihood (of the risk materializing)
5 Critical Immediate financial impact, recovery costs, loss of opportunity more than 20% of a project's budget/benefits impacted.	**4 Probable** more than 1 in 10 chance, or imminent
4 Severe direct financial impact, recovery costs, or loss of opportunity more than 20% of a project's budget/benefits impacted.	**3 Possible** less than 1 in 10 chance, or could happen within 1 year
3 Significant direct financial impact, recovery costs, or loss of opportunity between 10% and 20% of a project's budget/benefits impacted.	**2 Unlikely** less than 1 in 100 chance
2 Moderate direct financial impact, recovery costs, or loss of opportunity between 5% and 10% of a project's budget/benefits impacted.	**1 Remote** less than 1 in 1000 chance
1 Minor direct financial impact, recovery costs, or loss of opportunity less than 5% of a project's budget/benefits impacted.	

Figure 6.2 Likelihood and impact of risk

importance and to help focus subsequent analysis on the most significant risks.

During the kick-off phase also the project team needs to define activities and work streams.

Using a RACI template (see Figure 6.5) is helpful in establishing for each activity who is:

- Responsible = R –'doer'. These are the individuals who perform an activity – who are responsible for action/implementation. The account-able person defines the degree of responsibility. R status can be shared.

- Accountable = A – 'The buck stops here'. This is the individual who is ultimately accountable – includes yes/no and power of veto. Only one A can be assigned to an activity/decision.

- To be consulted = C – 'in the loop'. These are individuals who need to be consulted prior to a decision or action being taken. Two-way communi-cation is vital in all forms of consultation.

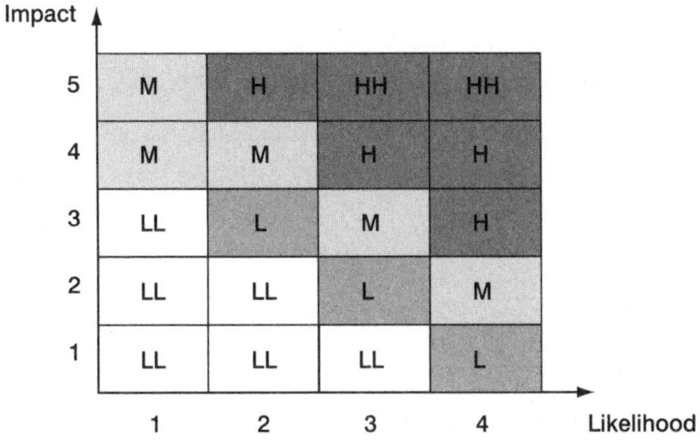

Impact	1	2	3	4
5	M	H	HH	HH
4	M	M	H	H
3	LL	L	M	H
2	LL	LL	L	M
1	LL	LL	LL	L

Likelihood

HH	**Business Critical**
	Immediate action should be taken to reduce the risk.

H	**Major/immediate threats to the programme/project**
	Immediate action should be taken to reduce the risk.

M	**Serious threats to the programme/project**
	Early action is required to reduce the risk.

L	**Moderate threats to the programme/project**
	Actions to deal with risks should be planned

LL	**Low-level threats to the programme/project**
	The least significant risks, with little impact.

Risks should be periodically monitored to confirm their status.

Figure 6.3 Risk matrix

Risk Ref	Risk Description	Status (Open/closed)	Original Risk Evaluation			Date raised	Owner	Planned actions	Target resolution date	Actions complete
			Impact (1–5)	Likelihood (1–4)	Risk mapping (HH–LL)					

Figure 6.4 Risk log

Task	Activity	Required by date	Responsible	Accountable	Consult	Inform

Figure 6.5 RACI template

- To be informed = I – 'for your information'. These are the individuals who need to be informed after decisions or actions are taken. One-way communication is sufficient for this.

A RACI chart can be used in conjunction with another useful planning tool: a Gantt chart. This is a diagram used for illustrating the sequence of events involved in achieving a project plan. It is made by representing events as blocks on a picture whose horizontal axis is divided into units of time. It enables project managers and team members to assess the tasks that need to be done, the sequence of those tasks and progress to date.

To create a Gantt chart:

1. Decide on the tasks involved in the project being undertaken.

2. Through experience or discussion, decide on the likely duration of each task.

3. Work out the sequence of activities.

4. Establish the overall project deadline.

5. Draw the Gantt chart. (There are versions of this available on software such as Microsoft Project).

6. Monitor progress against the planned activity.

Building a house

	Week 12	Week 13	Week 14	Week 15	Week 16	Week 17	Week 18
Dig foundations	▓						
Concrete foundations		▓					
Lay bricks			▓▓				
Fit windows					▓		
Fit roof timbers					▓		
Felt and tile roof						▓	
Fit electrical system					▓		
Fit plumbing system						▓	
Plaster walls						▓	
Finish fittings							▓

Figure 6.6 Gantt chart

Delivery

During the delivery phase of the project the project team needs to control risks and issues and make any changes to the project plan that occur as well as monitoring delivery against the plan.

Review

Remember to recognize and celebrate success as well as capturing the learning for future projects.

7

What is spiritual intelligence (SQ)?

The last chapter established the need for BQ to anticipate and drive change and this chapter focuses on SQ. The following areas are covered:

- What is SQ?
- How can SQ help in times of change?
- How do you identify SQ and how do you develop it?
- Creating your personal vision.
- Creating your personal values.
- Creating organizational vision and values and the behaviours that bring the values to life.

Specifically this chapter:

- explores the meaning of SQ
- looks at the pathway to SQ.

DEFINING SQ

Whereas BQ, PQ and to a degree EQ are tangible, SQ is less so. Our understanding of SQ and application of it depends upon our own personal values, our motivation to explore this territory, our own level of self-awareness and our ability and willingness to 'let go'.

SQ at work is embodied in the display of values such as integrity, honesty, responsibility, compassion, respect and courage. It is often about exploring questions rather than having answers and allows us to feel comfortable with uncertainty and inconsistency. Leaders such as Gandhi and Mandela embody high levels of SQ. They embodied a sense of purpose and integrity that surmounted many difficulties.

SQ is the intelligence that allows our EQ, PQ and BQ to function effectively. It is the intelligence that allows us to approach issues intuitively and helps us to assess and make the choice that is right or more significant than any other.

Whereas PQ and BQ are about knowing and doing, SQ is about being – how we are (see figure 7). Being is about demonstrating your true self, allowing your identity and purpose to shine through in a way that is attractive and potentially inspiring for others. Leaders such as Anita Roddick, founder of the Body Shop, and designer and businessman Terence Conran, of Conran fame, have a strong sense of identity that is echoed in their brands.

People with strong SQ look after the whole self – the mind, the body and the soul. This can explain the growing need and popularity for alternative therapies and activities such as meditation, hypnotherapy, aromatherapy, reiki and yoga. It is an indication of our realization that the whole self needs to be cared for and be congruent in order for us to give of our best from ourselves.

Evidence that this is not being encouraged as much as it should be in the workplace is shown in a recent study by HR consultants Watson Wyatt. They found that the number of people who say they are happy at work has fallen from 25 per cent to 7 per cent over recent years. People account for up to 85 per cent of an organization's overheads but their value as an intangible asset far exceeds this cost.

There is a growing disillusionment today in organizations that have a singular focus on profit and lack of contribution to society. A growing trend has emerged in the workplace for people to seek spiritual meaning, to work for and deal with organizations whose values and beliefs tie in with their own and who have integrity. Witness the popularity of such ethical brands

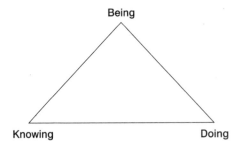

Figure 7.1 Knowing, doing, being

as Fair Trade and the Cooperative Bank and the growth of corporate social responsibility.

Business in the Community, established in 1982, report that companies that behave responsibly in the community perform better on the bottom line. It has become increasingly important that businesses are seen to be socially responsible, to be seen to be concerned about the environment and to act in a way that benefits local communities. However, stakeholders easily see through businesses that make politically correct statements and give out the right messages but who do not do so with integrity. The erosion of public trust in corporations has been fuelled by the collapse and loss of billions of pounds of shareholder value by such companies as Marconi and Cable & Wireless as well as the impact of the Enron and Parmalat scandals. Too little challenge in the boardroom is seen to be the root of many governance failures.

UK insurance company Legal & General (L&G) has established a strong reputation for its effective corporate governance over many years, and it was one of the strongest critics of BSkyB's actions in appointing James Murdoch as the new chief executive there. Some observers credit L&G's robust corporate culture to work that was instigated by the previous chairman, the late Sir Christopher Harding (Chairman 1994–99).

Reviews of board performance were introduced under Harding, and have continued with his successor, Rob Margetts, who is Non-Executive Chairman (as was Harding). 'They have made measuring performance a key part of the way they do business,' says one executive who knows the company well (quoted in an article entitled 'The Unusual Suspects' by Stefan Stern in *Human Resources* published in January 2002): 'Every part of the business has targets, including the board, and non-executives are no different. The board's performance as a whole is measured, not just the work of individuals.'

In times of change applying SQ can make the difference between a successful and a speedy transition and an unsuccessful change and a prolonged and painful transition.

SQ is not about finding religious beliefs, although that can form part of the way in which we reach and attain spiritual development. SQ is the place we go to in our minds where we attain clarity of thought, where there are no interruptions and where rational thinking is not invited. SQ allows us to rise above our ego and overcome the self-centredness and ambition that goes with that and exchange it for a deeper understanding of oneself, a stronger sense of meaning and purpose and a more courageous approach to everything we do.

In times of change it can be all too tempting to rely on the rational, conscious mind to deal with the inevitable problems and questions that arise either for you or for others. This is why 'letting go' and not 'thinking' about these issues is so important. Sometimes less is more and when we are about to enter a state of panic or chaos that change has provoked, this is the very time that we should trust our intuition, trust who we are and be courageous with our creativity in addressing those issues guided by our inner resources.

Danah Zohar set out some pointers on criteria for high SQ:

- Be flexible.
- Be self-aware.
- Have a vision and be led by your values.
- Learn from experience of adversity.
- Look for connections.
- Value diversity.
- Stand up for what you believe in.
- Question and reframe a problem.
- Don't let position or status go to your head.

Someone who had to draw on all his inner strength, intuition and courage, following one of the biggest tragedies of our time, 9/11, was Rudolph Guiliani, former New York City mayor. In an article entitled 'Humility is the key to leadership' by Jennifer Schramm, published in _People Management_ on 11 July 2002, Guiliani is quoted as saying: 'A leader is someone who has a philosophy, has thought it out and tested it. Key to leadership is not hiding areas of weakness but showing humility'.

THE PATHWAY TO CREATING SQ

The management behaviourist Abraham Maslow's work can help us further explore and understand the meaning of SQ. Abraham Maslow (1954) talked about self-actualization in his hierarchy of needs model. People whose needs for self-actualization (the need for meaning and purpose in their lives) have been met display strong SQ in achieving this.

In his hierarchy of needs Maslow describes people's needs as follows:

- physiological – the need for food and water;
- safety – the need for shelter, security and freedom from danger;
- belonging – the need for identification and acceptance amongst others;
- esteem – the need to be recognized by others and feel good about self;
- self-actualization – the need for meaning and purpose in your life.

Maslow states that the lower-order needs are dominant until satisfied, which is when the higher-order needs come into operation, therefore he claimed that starving people in need of food and water will sacrifice other needs such as freedom to obtain food – and only when needs at one level of the hierarchy are met will people switch their attention to the next need up the hierarchy.

Figure 7.2 Maslow's hierarchy of needs

If our safety needs are met we move onto satisfying our 'belonging' needs. The need to belong often happens as much outside the family as inside it. People want to identify with their peers inside and outside work. They join clubs where they have something in common with others, for example Mums cultivate relationships with other Mums they meet at school. This action is often driven by an unconscious need to belong. Work may form the focus of our belonging life and leaders of change can use people's need for belonging to real advantage in trying to create a team with a single vision.

Maslow saw esteem needs in two ways – the need for esteem from others as well as the need for self-esteem. Gaining esteem from others may involve trying to prove oneself – for example in organizations where departments compete against each other for the bonus or the glory rather than the greater need of the organization's goal.

Often those who work hardest to gain recognition from others lack self-esteem. If the organization is seen to promote this culture of competitiveness, it is doing little to allow its people to move up the ladder of needs towards self-actualization. In fact, it is creating a vicious cycle of people continually searching for esteem and not rising above that. This is not helpful when change needs to happen in organizations as change can increase people's need for esteem.

Having high self-esteem means that you are comfortable with who you are and you are not dependent on the opinions of others. If self-esteem is high, the need to realize one's true potential increases.

As mentioned earlier, the ability for people to reach self-actualization (to find meaning and purpose in their life) in the workplace is challenging given that the systems, politics and cultures work against self-actualization rather than for it. Increasingly, therefore, employees' psychological contract with their employers is changing and people are looking for greater meaning in life outside work.

In her book 'The Divine Right of Capital', Marjorie Kelly says:

The system we have in this country around the management of money does not create spiritually aware organizations.

- Employees are viewed as property – they buy and sell properties which have employees and they can dispose of them how they see fit.
- Employees are seen as a liability on the balance sheet.
- Employees are minimally paid to keep profitability up _but if you remove employees the company has no value._

With a billion people in the developing world living on less than a dollar a day, there is a growing frustration with the yawning wealth gap. It is often not clear to people or even seen as a priority to create understanding of the part they play or the meaning and purpose of what they are doing in the greater context of the organization.

One project that has been successful in creating this understanding is the Eden Project. The Eden Project is an example of a 'social enterprise' – it draws nearly two million visitors a year to what, five years ago, was a sterile clay-pit in Cornwall. The local environment has benefited from a 5 per cent increase in employment. One of the aims of the project is to demonstrate that unconventional approaches based on ethics can make sense in a commercial world. In an article entitled 'Theories of Creation' by John Bessant, Julie Birkinshaw and Rick Delbridge, published in _People Management_ in February 2004, Eden's founder and chief executive Tim Smit explains: 'The epiphany in doing what I do is understanding that public servants, bankers and lawyers are just people. If you cut through the traditional rules of engagement and fire up people with the power of your ideas, it is remarkable how they will start to take ownership of those ideas and change the way they engage with you in order to help.'

In times of change in particular, exercising SQ and creating that meaning and purpose for people will:

- allow them to understand how they are contributing to the greater good;
- help them buy-in to the change;
- help them promote the change;
- potentially increase the likelihood of meeting their esteem needs and self-actualization needs.

Over the years there have been many challenges to Maslow's work. Whitmore (1997) describes how Viktor Frankl, author of _Man's Search for Meaning_ and a prisoner in a Nazi concentration camp during the Second World War, challenged Maslow's theory. He writes that none of the prisoners' basic survival needs were met (ie needs for food, water, shelter or safety) but 'those who gave away even what little they had tended to survive better than those who stole extra. They had found meaning in helping others and that in turn gave them the strength or the purpose for survival.'

How does this all link to leaders managing change more effectively? It implies that when there is a crisis or a state of uncertainty during a change, we can rise above our basic needs if we no longer think solely of ourselves but the greater good of the whole.

In later chapters we will look at what leaders need to do to increase their SQ and sustain this clarity of meaning and the drive and congruence that goes with it.

8

How SQ can help in times of change

This chapter investigates:

- the stages we go through when we experience a change that takes us away from 'normality';
- at which stages during the transition curve it is helpful for us to exercise strong SQ;
- the benefits for individuals and the organization of strong SQ during change.

THE STAGES OF CHANGE

In the 1960s psychologist Elizabeth Kubler-Ross identified the stages people move through during grief and loss. Change evokes a similar cycle of emotional responses. The Transition Curve, identified by her, and its application to business change, is based on the work of Laurence Peter and Rosabeth Moss Kanter, who describe the stages we go through when we experience change.

Figure 8.1 indicates how the stages in the transition curve affect our productivity and competence.

The 'shock' stage increases competence and productivity: one way of dealing with trauma is to throw ourselves into our work. When 'denial' hits, our competence takes a large dip as self-doubt and lack of confidence and self-esteem take over.

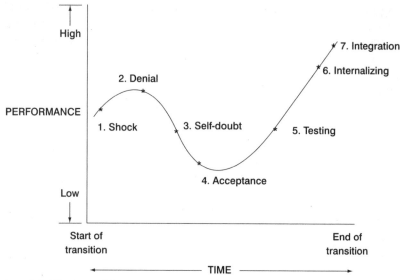

Figure 8.1 The transition curve

At 'acceptance' we have reached the lowest point in our competence before the acceptance of the reality helps us try out the new regime. As we begin to 'test' and 'internalize' the change our competence and confidence increase beyond what it was and reach a new level by the time we arrive at 'integration'.

WHEN TO DISPLAY STRONG SQ

During which stages of the transition curve will it be important for you to display strong SQ?

It may be helpful to investigate the reasons why people react the way they do during change, that will identify the implications of what might happen and what SQ tactics you need to be adopting.

Shock, denial and self-doubt can be created by:

- lack of understanding around why the change has happened – 'It doesn't mean anything to me';

- not being fully aware of the implications of the change – 'I might lose my job' (therefore threatening safety and belonging needs);

- realizing the implications of the change – 'My power base will be taken away', 'I will have to work in a different area and I will lose my colleagues/friends';

- lack of buy-in to the change either because it has been imposed or the person fundamentally disagrees with it;

- discomfort with having to do something that the person is either not comfortable with or not competent at.

Managing the above outcomes will call for the use of strong SQ. Why? – because people's self-esteem may be low; people may find it hard to understand the meaning and purpose of the change. By applying high SQ during shock, denial and self-doubt, you are likely to facilitate the movement of people through the last four stages of the transition curve more effectively and in a timely manner.

So what are the characteristics of the last four stages: acceptance, testing, internalizing and integration and what are you likely to see?:

- Rules will be changing, which may result in lack of confidence and a reversion to self-doubt.

- There will be uncertainty because the answer to the problem or the best solution is not known.

- There is clarity around what the change is, but not necessarily about what the future holds.

- There is an increase in activity and energy as new behaviours are tried out.

- There will be a sharing of ideas with others around how to make it work.

- Confidence and self-esteem increase as the positive aspects of change are noticed.

To manage this situation there is a need for creativity, intuition, vision, compassion and an ability to let go. Applying these qualities will benefit you on your journey through change as well as those you are leading.

THE NEED FOR MEANING AND PURPOSE

When change is happening at work, leaders and team members may well be asking: 'What's going on? What is my role in all of this?' During change people often ask themselves whether they are following their true purpose when they come to work or simply going through the motions to get a wage packet. Finding our true purpose allows us to express who we are, at work and outside.

Imagine you are a natural backstroke swimmer and you are asked to compete with the freestyle swimmers. You might be able to make it through the competition but it would be a strain. It would not be a seamless or beautiful experience because freestyle is not your forte – not an expression of who you truly are. It can be the same with work.

Dean Spitzer, author of 'Super motivation' talks about the eight desires or motivators that we all need to be met in varying degrees. These eight desires are shown in Figure 8.2. During change the need for these motivators or desires to be met increases significantly, particularly the needs for competence and meaning.

SPITZER'S EIGHT MOTIVATORS/DESIRES	DEFINITIONS
Activity	People want to be active and involved. In our personal lives most people avoid boredom and monotony. Yet at work employees are expected to accept boring, repetitive, monotonous jobs without complaint.
Ownership	Owning things makes people feel better about themselves. 'Psychological' ownership is even more important than 'physical' ownership. Employees want to psychologically own their work. They want input into their work and want to feel responsible for their jobs.
Power	People want to control their destiny. They don't want to feel powerless over external forces shaping their lives. With fewer top–down, control organizations more and more employees are demanding their freedom back.
Affiliation	People are social creatures. They like to interact and socialize with one another although the degree of sociability will vary. Social support and helping relationships are among the many benefits provided by work.
Competence	This is the core of self-esteem. People welcome opportunities to feel more competent. Work can provide these opportunities.
Achievement	It is important for us to succeed at something. Under the right conditions, employees will be willing to work hard and overcome obstacles to achieve a goal.
Recognition	People want to feel appreciated by others and be positively recognized for their efforts. Recognition is a powerful force which has the capability to unleash energy and motivation.
Meaning	People want a reason for doing something. They want reassurance that their efforts, however small, are making a difference.

Figure 8.2 Based on the work of Dean Spitzer

In order to satisfy meaning, leaders have to show people the significance of their work and provide a vision. Why? The human need to find meaning in whatever we do and experience will be highest in times of change as we search to make sense of what is happening. We have a desire to see our lives in some larger context that gives meaning. We have a need to aspire to something that gives us and our actions a sense of worth. Your ability to do this will be an inspiration to those around you and will create further motivation for the change.

Frankl (1984) wrote: 'Our search for meaning is the primary motivation in our lives. It is this search that makes us the spiritual creatures that we are. And it's when this deep need for meaning goes unmet that our lives come to feel shallow or empty.' This can account for the dip in competence that is illustrated in the transition curve. (See Figure 8.1).

An example of an organization that has tried to model the workplace in terms of providing meaning is Semco (a manufacturer of pumps, mixers, valves and other industrial equipment based in Brazil). In their tape 'Spiritual approaches to energising your company', Corinne McLaughlin and Gordon Davidson talk about Semco's success. Its President, Ricardo Semler, in the past voted Latin-American Businessman of the Year, describes how he runs his business: workers make the decisions normally made by their bosses, all employees are treated as responsible adults and most set their own working hours. They have access to company records and vote on important company decisions. Most of the managerial staff set their own salaries and bonuses. Semler writes:

> To survive in modern times a company must have an organizational structure that accepts change as its basic premise, lets tribal customs thrive, and fosters a power that is derived from respect, not rules. In other words, the successful companies will be the ones that put quality of work first. Do this and the rest – quality of product, productivity of workers, profits for all will follow.

> We give people an opportunity to test, question and disagree. You let them come and go as they please, work at home if they want, set their own salaries, and choose their own bosses. We let them change their minds and ours, prove us wrong when we are wrong, make us humbler. Such a system relishes change.

Another example of a company who believes much its success can be attributed to giving people meaning is Dell Computers. Dell (1999) says that change is a daily occurrence at Dell Computers and to help his company deal with that, he not only has a common goal but has an organizational philosophy which is 'stay allergic to hierarchy'. Dell Computers is organized into small teams who have total autonomy and accountability and are not permitted to grow too large. Every team is held accountable for its financial and customer service results and each of those team members is rewarded with share options in the company.

These examples demonstrate how letting go of unnecessarily rigid controls and creating an environment that allows meaning for people can benefit everyone. The next chapter looks at further advantages of SQ in the organization and how you can better develop your SQ.

9

Identifying and developing SQ

This chapter will:

- look at what organizations achieve from applying SQ;
- offer examples of businesses that have benefited from SQ;
- provide you with a questionnaire to identify your own SQ.

BENEFITS OF SQ IN ORGANIZATIONS

In recent years, we have been bombarded by news of the collapse of well-known organizations because of fraudulent or unethical dealings. It is becoming increasingly important for stakeholders to ensure that the organizations they deal with operate morally and ethically and that they have a code of conduct that is founded on a strong set of incorruptible values. A bishop in the UK recently even suggested that a member of the clergy should sit on the board of all major companies to act as the 'moral conscience' of the organization.

There is a belief that if SQ becomes the norm, organizations will achieve such benefits as:

- a sense of relevance and purpose to people's lives;
- a better work ethic and work/life balance;
- a greater respect for diversity;

- lower stress;
- less ego, conflict and gossip;
- less inappropriate competitiveness;
- more mentoring and supportiveness;
- higher levels of creativity and innovation;
- lower levels of fraud and theft;
- a better respect for and conservation of resources.

The rapid amount of change in organizations means that the need to develop our anchors is greater, and organizations need to respond to a changing world. This has created a growing hunger for spiritual development. People are becoming curious about many different approaches to finding their purpose and meaning, exploring different religions, meditation or hypnosis. These approaches fuel a capacity for everything to be questioned.

REASONS WHY SQ HAS BECOME SO IMPORTANT

We live in a time when many people feel that there are no universally agreed and definite 'goalposts' any more, no clear boundaries, no shared values, no accepted way to grow up, and no agreed understanding of responsibility. People are searching for answers to important questions. This indicates a desire to find and use SQ.

As there is a need to increase spiritual meaning in our lives to deal with what is going on in our world, businesses and organizations have to accommodate this search for purpose. This means that if organizations wish to be successful, they must integrate people's spiritual needs into working lives. People are beginning to question their jobs and what they derive from them; unfulfilling work begs the question: is this all there is?

As a consequence, organizations are having to clarify and redefine their purpose and their values, so that they can offer meaning to everyone who works there. Meaning, as we saw in Maslow's hierarchy of needs (see Chapter 7) is a primary driver, which implies that people will not contribute effectively to their organization without it.

SQ AND CREATIVITY

Creative working environments can be very satisfying for individuals. There is a link between 'letting go', using one's intuition and creativity and innovation. Often individuals find it difficult to be creative within an organizational environment because:

- There is an unspoken demand to 'follow the rules'.
- People are afraid to appear the fool.
- People have a tendency to look for one 'right' answer.
- We are afraid of taking risks.
- We are trained from school to use our 'left brain'. Logical thinking predominates at work rather than 'right brain' thinking.
- There is little time at work to 'daydream' or think creatively.

One company that believes in allowing creativity in the workplace and has benefited enormously from its courage to do so is Dyson. Dyson spent five years working through over 5,000 prototypes before settling on the final bagless vacuum cleaner design. As Art Fry of 3M famously observed: 'You have to kiss a lot of frogs to find your prince.' Results of innovation can take time to incubate. The Sara Lee coffee business, Douwe Egberts, launched its Decathlon innovation programme in 1995, and the first blockbuster success to emerge from it, the Senseo coffee machine, reached the market in 2002.

In order to foster a climate of creativity people need time and the freedom to think and challenge the status quo. This takes a high degree of SQ from the individual and encouragement and permission from the organization to try the new and different.

BT Brightstar had its origins in a conversation in 1999 between Stewart Davies, chief executive of Exact Technologies, BT's research and development (R&D) business, and Harry Berry, a 30-year veteran of BT. Davies' challenge was to make the R&D more commercially oriented.

Berry and Davies started looking into new ways of unlocking value. They began sounding out external partners for funding and commercial expertise and they began looking for ways of shaking up the traditional culture of the laboratories.

The initial changes were purely symbolic. Berry refused an office; instead, he made his home in a large communal area next to the coffee machines and encouraged people to 'drop in' to discuss any ideas they had. The counter-cultural style was immediately noticed and soon Berry was inundated with new ideas. This gave Berry sufficient ideas, exciting technologies, market opportunities and frustrated entrepreneurs to launch Brightstar.

First he created an incubator. External venture capitalists were brought into the company and their expertise was used to vet the ideas and provide seed funding. A 2,000-strong club of local support services was brought on site to help with legal and financial matters. An advisory board was created to decide which ideas were worth turning into small businesses.

From its launch in February 2000 to the end of that year, the incubator launched four businesses and funded a further 11. Over time, a multi-phase process was put in place, from the discovery phase where scientists pitched their informal concepts to Berry's team, through incubation, where the team was put together and the business plan developed, and into the accelerator where the focus switched to product development and client acquisition.

By 2001, 330 ideas had been presented and four businesses with third-party backing had been established, with total revenues of £30 million. But as the dot.com bust took hold, BT Brightstar was hit by lack of external venture capital funding for its business.

There was no more money forthcoming from BT, so in January 2003 the company sold a 60 per cent stake in Brightstar to private equity firm Coller Capital. This model provided Brightstar with long-term stability, as well as access to a set of related business ventures that Coller had bought from Lucent the year before. (Details taken from an article entitled 'Theories of creation' by John Bessant, Julian Birkinshaw and Rick Delbridge, published in _People Management_ in February 2004.)

THE LEARNING ORGANIZATION

People with high levels of SQ are often good learners. They are not afraid to take a stand, they are in touch with themselves and comfortable with who they are. This intelligence is a form of liberation which allows people to break away from unnecessary organizational constraints and habits.

Many artists and creative people, such as poets and singers, demonstrate SQ. Organizations with high levels of SQ encourage creativity and innovation. They foster a climate that encourages learning and challenge.

In 1993, Zeneca demerged from ICI before merging with Swedish-based firm Astra in 1999. The joining of Astra and Zeneca was hailed as 'the combination of two companies with similar science-based cultures and a shared vision of the pharmaceutical industry.' Creating a truly integrated culture for everyone in the firm was not as simple. 'It's relatively easy at board level to say how well these companies fit together strategically,' said Malcolm Hurrell, Vice-President of HR (UK), 'but getting people at all levels to let go of things they liked and embrace a new company, the new culture: that was the real challenge.'

Learning and development has been important in creating the new organization. Innovation underpins the company's products, particularly R&D. 'Creativity is essential,' says Hurrell, in an article entitled 'Look on the Sunny Side' by Carol Glover, published in _People Management_ on 18 April 2002. 'Other pharmaceutical companies may be doing the same thing but being successful is about how well you execute things and how creative you are at the edges to demonstrate the expertise ...The most important thing in fostering creativity is to have a culture of learning. Unless we look at the learning environment, intervention itself won't make much of an impact.'

The London School of Economics (LSE) encourages its staff as well as its students to learn new skills. Every staff member with an annual salary below £19,000 is eligible for the 'Learn for You' scheme introduced last year.

This includes employees at the sharp end, such as those sweating it out in the kitchens. LSE will put £150 towards the cost of any course employees choose as long as it has nothing to do with their job. Lorraine Clark, induction champion at LSE, says the scheme has made a tremendous difference to motivating low-paid staff. They have used the money for driving lessons, a course on make-up, pottery, horticulture, tennis and horse-riding. As Helen Thompson, a cashier at LSE, remarks: 'It makes you feel good. ' (Taken from an article entitled 'Every Incentive' by Suzy Bashford, published in *Human Resources* in January 2004.)

EXAMPLES OF SQ IN ORGANIZATIONS

McLaughlin (1994) uses the following examples to show the benefits of a spiritual approach in the workplace:

- Apple Computers pay their employees to use the 'quiet ' room for 30 minutes every day in order to develop their creativity and intuition. The company is hoping that this will create the opportunity for people to access a higher level of consciousness that is greater than rational thinking.

- Aaron Feurenstein is the CEO of Malden Mills, a company which makes polar fleece fabrics in Lawrence, Massachusetts. A few years ago, three out of his four factories burnt down and he made the decision to keep all of his 3,000 employees on the payroll because he held a belief that the labour force is the best asset a company has. As a result, the employees helped him rebuild the premises and within one year all the factories were up and running again.

- Taco Bell and Pizza Hut hire chaplains to come into the workplace to help employees with their problems. This has reduced turnover rate massively.

INCREASING YOUR SQ

Complete the following questionnaire to help you assess your SQ.

Rate yourself on a scale of 1 to 5:

1 = I don't do/believe this at all

2 = I do/believe this infrequently

3 = I do/believe this some of the time

4 = I do/believe this often

5 = I do/believe this all the time.

Assessing your SQ

I am respectful of other people's thoughts and feelings

I find it easy to admit when I am wrong

I have a vision of where I want to be

I am open to diversity and differences in others

I am not afraid to look inward and see my limitations

I am OK about feeling uncomfortable

My actions are for the long-term good of others

I use adversity to identify what I can learn about myself

I know my meaning and purpose in life

I believe that behind every action that someone takes there is a positive intention

I have the courage of my convictions

I know what I contribute to those around me

I forgive other people if they have done wrong

I know the truth about myself without being told

I can live in a state of uncertainty without knowing all the answers

I give my time, money or material resources to help others

I know who I am and what I stand for

I put events in a larger context to understand their significance

I accept life and people as they are presented to me without wanting to change them

I actively seek to understand my deepest motivations

I stand alone against others in my work/family if their actions threaten my integrity

My goal in life is to act with compassion

I recognize my strengths and weaknesses

I live my life with optimism

I listen intently with the motivation of understanding another's viewpoint

I find it easy to disclose personal things about myself to others

I act in a way that is consistent with my values

I feel positively about myself in spite of my shortcomings

I know what is important to me

I know why I am here on earth

ASPECTS OF SQ

We have identified three important aspects of SQ: acceptance, self-identity and purpose and values. Our definitions of each follow:

- **Acceptance**:
    - the ability to love, respect and forgive others despite what they have said or done;
    - the ability to love yourself despite your shortcomings;
    - valuing diversity and difference.
- **Self-identity**:
    - having a deep knowledge and acceptance of yourself, who you are, and what you stand for, what your strengths and weaknesses are;
    - allowing yourself to be yourself;
    - trusting yourself.
- **Purpose and values**:
    - having clarity about your purpose, value and contribution to the world;
    - understanding how you fit into the bigger picture, having a strong sense of meaning;
    - being congruent in your values and actions;
    - being brave and facing your fears.

Please transfer your scores from the questionnaire onto the table below.

Add up each column and you will receive a score for each category. AC stands for acceptance, SI stands for self-identity, and PV stands for purpose and values.

AC	SI	PV
Q1	Q2	Q3
Q4	Q5	Q6
Q7	Q8	Q9
Q10	Q11	Q12
Q13	Q14	Q15
Q16	Q17	Q18
Q19	Q20	Q21
Q22	Q23	Q24
Q25	Q26	Q27
Q28	Q29	Q30
TOTAL FOR AC:	TOTAL FOR SI:	TOTAL FOR PV:

Scores between 50 and 35 represent a high SQ score for that category so continue doing what you are doing.

Scores between 34 and 20 represent an average SQ score for that category. This could be improved by following some of the tactics described below for increasing your SQ.

Scores between 19 and 10 represent a low SQ score for that category. We strongly recommend that this could be improved by following some of the approaches described below for increasing your SQ.

PRACTICAL THINGS TO DO TO DEVELOP SQ

The following are suggestions on what you can do to develop your SQ further. Some of the activities will be more appealing to you than others depending on the stage of development you are at in relation to the three criteria. While these activities can be carried out at any time, they are particularly beneficial during times of change as this is usually when relationships and thinking are more challenged!

Acceptance

- Select the relationship you would most like to improve. Look at the areas where you score lowest in your self-assessment and identify what you could use from those to apply to this relationship.
- Are there people you are neglecting or over-nurturing? What can you do to correct the balance?
- What are you doing to create a cooperative, supportive and trusting environment with equal degrees of concern for everyone?
- What do you have in place that shows you have the spiritual well-being of your employees as a priority?
- What are you doing that shows that your own spiritual well-being is a priority?
- Identify one action that you can take with your team at work to show them that you are open to diversity and differences in others.
- Choose a current problem or unmade decision that you have. What would have to happen for you to make progress with this? What can you do to make sure the decision will be for the highest long-term good of others?
- If you were to adopt the belief that behind every action there is a positive intention, how would you have dealt differently with the last 'inappropriate' action your team member, colleague or manager took?
- Think of a time when you were in a disagreement/argument with someone that was not resolved. What were you doing to create that situation, how could you better tune into the thoughts and feelings of the other individual?

- What positive action can you take to share more of your time, money and resources with others?

Self-identity

- What have you done to show others that you are not always right and what you have learnt as a result of that?

- Find someone with whom you would not normally feel comfortable engaging in conversation. Take an active interest in what he or she is saying and write down what you have learnt about yourself and what behaviours you used when listening to the person that were different from your usual behaviours.

- Dedicate a time slot each week to identifying the strengths and weaknesses you have displayed both professionally and personally. List the impact of each and what you have learnt as a result.

- Share your strengths and weaknesses with your team/family and get their feedback.

- Identify one situation in the last six months when you did not have the courage of your convictions to do what you wanted to do. Identify the reasons why and what you could do differently next time.

- How well do your immediate team/friends/family know you? What can you do to let them know who you really are?

- What decisions have you made in the last six months that have been based on your intuition rather than reason and logic? Make an agreement with yourself to trust your intuition the next time a tough decision has to be made, note the results of that and what you learnt about yourself during that process.

- Spend a day doing what you want to do and record how you felt and what you learnt about yourself.

- How do you treat yourself at the moment when you get things 'wrong' or make a mistake? What other way could you handle it that would make you feel better?

- Draw a picture that depicts who you are. Keep it on your desk and talk it through with your team/family.

Purpose and values

- Identify something you are passionate for, aspire to or dream of achieving. What have you done to realize this? Why have you not achieved it? How are you going to achieve it?

- Write in a notebook over the course of three days an answer to the question, 'What is important to me? ' At the end of the three days, ask yourself, 'Is how I spend my time reflective of what is important to me?'

- Complete the visioning and values exercise in Chapters 10 and 11 and communicate what you have written to your team/family.

- In what ways have you communicated your purpose/vision to those you work with? How could this be more motivating for them?

- What have you done to communicate to those around you what your values are and how they link to your purpose/vision?

- Think of a time when you agreed to something that did not align to your values or you did not feel comfortable with. Why did you agree to it? What would need to happen for you to stand up and be counted for what you most value?

- What are your current goals and what are you doing to achieve those?

- What three things will you do over the next month to increase the levels of happiness you can create for yourself and others?

- What behaviours are you using that are allowing your employees to take the initiative confidently and learn from their experience?

- What are you doing that proves to your employees that your support for them is both consistent and long term?

The next chapters explore activities to increase your SQ and how this process can form part of organizational life.

10

Creating your personal vision

This chapter covers the following areas:

- What is a personal vision?
- Why is having a personal vision important?
- A process for creating your personal vision.

DEFINING A PERSONAL VISION

A vision is picture of a future state that is sufficiently compelling to inspire the individual to work towards achieving this state. As a leader during change you will have a greater sense of purpose and determination if you have a personal vision. Witness Martin Luther King's vision 'I have a dream' and President Kennedy's vision 'To put a man on the moon'.

Identifying your purpose and vision is a great step towards personal understanding and acceptance. By understanding your personal vision and accepting it you can devise a plan of how to live it out. This in turn will create inner happiness and satisfaction which you and others can benefit from. It will ultimately allow you to develop your SQ because without this knowledge it will be impossible for your life to be congruent.

As part of the tape 'Spiritual approaches to energising your company' Corinne McLaughlin and Gordon Davidson describe the personal vision of Tom Chappell. The founder of retailer Tom's of Maine, Tom decided that he wanted to go into the ministry and attended the Harvard Divinity School. It was while he was there that he realized that his purpose was not to express his spirituality in the pulpit but to do it through his company. He now creates products that are natural and valuable to others. He gives away 10 per cent of his pre-tax profits to charities and gives employees four paid hours a month to volunteer for community service.

WHY HAVING A PERSONAL VISION IS IMPORTANT

Psychologist and NLP practitioner Robert Dilts' logical levels model (see Figure 10.1) looks at the power of personal clarity of purpose because it allows you to challenge and change beliefs and to be consistent with that purpose. By knowing your direction you will be able to align your beliefs, values and behaviours.

When you have a personal vision of what you want to be or do, it will permeate the rest of your life. Dilts (1994) talks about this through describing levels. The purpose/spirituality level is at the top of his model. It influences the other levels of:

- identity;
- beliefs and values;
- capabilities and skills;
- behaviours;
- environment.

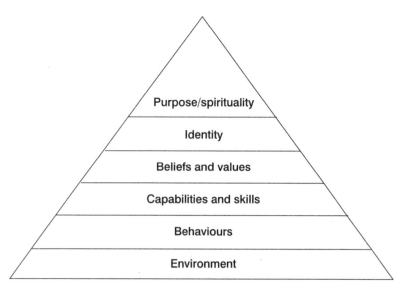

Figure 10.1 Dilts' logical levels

For example, if you know that your purpose is 'to create a better lifestyle for others', all of the other levels will align with that:

- Under 'identity' you would seek out a role that served that purpose, such as that of personal trainer.

- Your beliefs and values would align so that you might say 'I believe that by helping people get fitter they will have a better quality of life.'

- Your capabilities and skills will follow on from those beliefs, for example you will seek out training courses to become more effective in what you do.

- Your behaviours will align with that: you will work one-to-one with individuals giving them feedback on progress to achieve their fitness goals.

- The environment you create will fit with that. You will have the most appropriate equipment and location for your customers to achieve their best.

A good example of someone guided by her purpose was Anita Roddick of the Body Shop who built her soap factory in Glasgow because it was an area of high unemployment. She made the decision to employ the 'unemployable' and put 25 per cent of net profits back into the community.

FINDING YOUR PURPOSE

Often we are so busy with the day-to-day that we are not entirely clear what our purpose is, so it is useful to explore and examine the capabilities and skills you have, the beliefs you hold about yourself and the values you have. This process will assist you in clarifying your identity and purpose.

Finding your purpose during change is fundamental to the success of that change for you and for your people. Without it, you may feel uneasy or unsure and be unclear why.

IDENTIFYING YOUR PURPOSE

First, it is useful to identify what is truly important to you in life. A good starting place is to answer the following four questions as honestly as you can.

Answer the 'four big questions' below.
What have you got in life that you want?
What have you got in life that you don't want?
What haven't you got in life that you want?
What haven't you got in life that you don't want?

Make a list under each heading. Be honest with yourself. You may want to test your answers out with people who know you well.

Keep the answers to your four big questions to one side whilst you further explore your purpose using the following questions. As you answer the questions use the *present tense*.

Please feel free to amend the questions as you go if they are not entirely relevant to you. Please keep in mind the answers to the four big questions as these may help you as you progress through the further questions. These questions are based on Senge (1994).

- What is your ideal professional or vocational situation? What impact would you like your efforts to have?

- What material things would you like to own?

- If you could be exactly the kind of person you wanted, what would your qualities be?

- What would you like to create in the arena of individual learning, travel, reading, or any other activities?
- What is your ideal living environment?
- What is your vision for the community or society within which you live?
- What is your desire for health, fitness, athletics and anything to do with your body?
- What type of relationships would you like to have with friends, family and others?
- What else, in any other area of your life, would you like to create?
- Imagine that your life has a unique purpose – fulfilled through what you do, your relationships, and the way you live. Can you describe it as another reflection of your aspirations?

When you have completed all the questions, look back at your responses to the four big questions and make sure that your answers are aligned – check whether there is anything that conflicts, ask yourself why that is and make a decision on what you want it to be.

Using the answers to the questions above and the answers to the four big questions, fill in the statement below:

My purpose in life is to: ....

....

....

....

Now that you have answered the questions, represent your vision pictorially on a piece paper. Combine this phrase with the picture you have drawn and ask yourself if the two pieces of work lie congruently with you.

Ask yourself if this expresses what you want. If it does, find a meaningful location to display it. If it does not, go back through the questions and identify where the gap is between your pictorial representation and the answers to your questions until you have an expression of a vision/purpose that you can identify with and aspire to.

11

Creating your personal values

This chapter discusses what values are and how our personal values help us during change. In this chapter you will have an opportunity to identify your personal values and how they link to your personal vision.

PERSONAL VALUES AND HOW THEY HELP DURING CHANGE

Values are the principles and ideas that are of importance to you and by which you lead your life. Identifying your values will help you to understand who you really are, what is really important to you and will help you achieve the purpose and vision you have created for yourself.

Values are at the core of who we are and they are derived from many different sources, such as parents, schools, friends and our culture. While our values can change as we move through and experience life, many values remain constant.

IDENTIFYING YOUR PERSONAL VALUES

Identifying personal values is surprisingly hard to do. The exercise below will help you identify between your 'espoused' values and the 'actual' values you live by. In other words, if you are stating that one of your values is 'development' but you have done nothing in the last year to develop yourself or others, it may well be a value you aspire to, or have 'espoused' rather than a value that you live by – an 'actual' value. In order knowingly to move towards fufilment of your goals, you will need to benefit from identifying what your 'actual' values are and how aligned they are to your purpose.

The list below may help you pick out your values through pinpointing what is important to you. Using the list, and with the addition of any other values that are not mentioned below, tick, in any order, the things that are most important to you. You are looking for a minimum of eight values.

Achievement

Adventure

Challenge

Change

Competence

Creativity

Democracy

Development

Effectiveness

Excellence

Excitement

Fame

Freedom

Friendships

Having a family

Helping people

Honesty

Independence

Integrity

Involvement

Knowledge

Love

Loyalty

Meaningful work

Money

Openness

Power

Privacy

Promotion

Recognition

Relationships

Reputation

Responsibility

Security

Serenity

Stability

Status

Tranquillity

Truth

Wisdom

Working alone

Working with others

From the values ticked, select your top eight priorities.
Once you have done this elaborate on exactly what they mean to you. This will help you to identify and measure when these values are being met.

1. ....

2. ....

3. ....

4. ....

5. ....

6. ....

7. ....

8. ....

PRIORITIZING VALUES

When all eight values have been elicited, rank them in order of priority with 1 being most important and 8 being least important. If you have difficulty in deciding on priorities ask yourself the following questions to help:

- Of the above values, which is most important to you?
- Imagine that you already have … (one from the list of values prioritized). Of the values that are left, is … or … more important to you?
- Imagine that you already have … (one from the list of values prioritized), of the values that are left, if you couldn't have … but you could have …, would that be acceptable?

```
1................................................................................................................................

2................................................................................................................................

3................................................................................................................................

4................................................................................................................................

5................................................................................................................................

6................................................................................................................................

7................................................................................................................................

8................................................................................................................................
```

You have now identified in priority order what is most importance to you in life. Now look at your purpose again with your values and consider these questions:

- How well do these values complement your purpose?
- Which values do not complement your purpose?
- What do you want to change if there is lack of alignment between your purpose and values?
- When you are happy that they are aligned, how will you communicate your purpose and values to the people who are important to you?
- When will you review your purpose and values?
- How will you ensure that you can remain true to your values and purpose during change?
- How closely do your personal life and the organization you are working in fulfil your values for you?
- How important is it that your personal life and organization reflect your values?
- What do you want to do if either your personal life or the organization is not fulfilling your values?

By gaining clarity on your own purpose and values, you will be in a position as a leader during change to remain congruent in what you believe, do and say. It will help you base your decisions on that deeper self-knowledge. It will assist you in gaining respect and credibility, knowing more clearly what course of action to take.

12

Creating organizational vision and values and bringing them to life

This chapter looks at:

- why vision and values are helpful to organizations, particularly in times of change;
- a process for creating a company vision;
- a process for identifying company values;
- examples of how values have been defined in terms of behaviours in different organizations.

WHY VISION AND VALUES ARE HELPFUL DURING CHANGE

Having a clear organizational vision and a set of values benefits the organization in the same way as it does for individuals. The organizational vision and values are the SQ of the organization.

Intuit, based in California, is the market leader in personal finance software and its employee turnover rate is 13 per cent, half the Silicon Valley average. It attributes a substantial part of its success to its employees' belief in its vision and values. The employees put the vision and values into practice because they were personally involved in defining them. Intuit's values centre around 'Doing right by all our customers', by which they mean all customers, external, internal, business partners and shareholders.

An example of how Intuit's behaviours were driven by their values was highlighted in February 1995, when Scott Cook, the founder of the company, found out from the *San Francisco Chronicle* that a bug had been found in Intuit's TurboTax software programme. When he read this Cook was about to board an aircraft to Los Angeles but trusted his executive team to deal with the issue. True to their belief in 'Doing right by all our customers', the Intuit team took the following action within a 24-hour period. They offered to send a new copy of TurboTax to any customer who wanted it – even those who were not registered users and had only ever 'borrowed' a copy! They offered to pay any IRS penalties incurred by customers as a result of the bug.

Mike Newnham, Vice President of Business Solutions at telecommunications company Orange, explains the importance of an engaging corporate vision: 'communicating your vision is critical, whether you are leading a small entrepreneurial company or a large corporate.' An organizational vision should clearly state what the organization seeks to create in the future. It shows where the organization wants to go and what it will be like when it gets there. It should be aspirational and inspirational. The best visions are short and easy to understand. They engage people at all levels in the organization – employees, customers and other stakeholders.

Which of the following examples of organizational visions do you find memorable and inspirational?:

- healthcare organization: 'Taking care of the life in our hands';
- upmarket hotel chain: 'Discovery';
- entertainment group: 'Dream, Believe, Dare, Do';
- financial services organization: 'To be the first choice for customers and colleagues';
- card manufacturer and retailer: 'To enrich people's lives, help them express their feelings, celebrate occasions and enhance their relationships';
- logistics company: 'People, Customers, Profits'.

A vision allows people a focal point during change and gives some explanation as to why the changes are happening and how the change is a means of helping the organization achieve its future state. Values are the guiding principles of the organization. If values are embedded in the organization, they allow all other systems, processes and behaviours to fit together in the organization. An illustration of this is the people management process.

RECRUITMENT & SELECTION	PERFORMANCE MANAGEMENT & COACHING	SUCCESSION PLANNING & TALENT MANAGEMENT	TRAINING & DEVELOPMENT	REWARD & RECOGNITION
COMPETENCIES				
VALUES				
VISION				

Figure 12.1 Vision, values and people management

If you have a clear set of values, it can help inform your competencies, which in turn will inform the five key components of people development in organizations:

- recruitment and selection;
- performance management and coaching;
- succession planning and talent management;
- training and development;
- reward and recognition.

One organization with whom we worked had a vision of 'inspiring customers'. Its values were customer service, team work, integrity and learning. It developed a competency framework that embedded these four values into the desired skills and behaviours for all levels of employees. The values and competencies in turn contributed to the recruitment and selection process. They were the criteria against which performance was managed, promotion decisions were made and development offered. The values were also reinforced through a recognition scheme that gave credit to people who had delivered inspirational service.

Aligning reward to an emerging culture is important. When a change programme was initiated at Defence Aviation Repair Agency, Dara, once part of the MOD, change agents identified that the culture was hierarchical and risk-averse. It was clear that such a culture would not survive in a commercial environment. A new reward system, based on broad banding with an upfront pay rise in return for commitment to accepting the new culture replaced the inflexible pay and grading structure that Dara had inherited from the MOD. This helped to encourage change while still retaining employee's pride in the quality of their work and the importance they placed on the customer. (Source: an article entitled 'Creative Fusion' by Rosie Blau, published in *People Management* on 7 November 2002). Having established values and aligned processes will make change more manageable and effective as the foundations of the organization are steady as things above it move.

Claridge's hotel in London has undergone a transformation over the past five years. In 1998 staff turnover was 73 per cent, complaints were running high and there was one rule for managers and another for staff. Consulting staff was a radical departure from the 'command and control' style of leadership that had gone before. Employees created a vision of the future: 'To be the first choice for guests and employees by 2005' and a mission: 'To bring 100 years of tradition into the 21st century.' The issuing of written communication was banned and daily staff meetings now take place. A programme to show appreciation to staff was developed that included improving the working environment for employees as well as developing a reward and recognition scheme. This recognizes people who have gone above and beyond the call of duty for guests. They each receive a prize from a lucky dip. Prizes include a chauffeur driven car journey to work, and a night in the penthouse – which would cost a guest £3,850. In addition, at the end of the three-month probationary period each new employee is invited to stay at Claridge's. By valuing employees and adopting a more open leadership style, complaints have fallen dramatically, staff turnover has dropped to 16 per cent and room occupancy has increased by 15 per cent.

A PROCESS FOR DEVELOPING A VISION FOR AN ORGANIZATION

This section outlines a process that will help you create a vision for your organization. Rather than leaving the vision to be created by the senior team, our recommendation is that all levels of the organization have an opportunity to contribute to it. This creates greater buy-in and a sense of ownership.

This process was recently used successfully with one retailer we worked with in helping them to define their vision –'Making a difference.' Use of the questions below formed the agenda for a series of brainstorm meetings involving a sample of people from all levels of the organization. By holding such representative, participative meetings buy-in is more likely from all levels at an early point. Next, words generated from the brainstorm are grouped together to find common themes. The vision is a short, inspirational and memorable phrase that captures the essence of the responses. The questions that form the basis for this exercise are:

- What do we want our customers to say about us in the future?

- What do we want our customers to feel about us in the future?

- What do we want our customers to hear about us in the future?

- What do we want our employees to say/feel/hear about us in the future?
- What do we want other stakeholders to say/feel/hear about us in the future?
- What do we stand for as an organization?
- What is our core purpose?

Once the short, inspirational and memorable phrase has been captured, a period of testing needs to happen throughout the organization to ensure that the vision is relevant to all those involved. Team meetings or small focus groups are a useful method for doing this. It is important that people responsible for testing the proposed vision with their colleagues receive feedback on the proposed vision so that it can be amended to reflect everyone's views.

Once that feedback has been collated and acted upon, the vision should be reworked to reflect the feedback. The senior team are then in a position to make a decision on how best to reflect that in the final wording.

The next stage will be to communicate the vision to all of the organization in whatever way is most appropriate for your culture. Businesses often communicate their vision and values together so that they become more meaningful. Rather than just presenting the vision and values in written format, it is essential that they are communicated during change using a method that is as participative as possible. In this way the vision and values come to life and people better understand the need for change.

England rugby team coach Clive Woodward has been able to create an outstandingly successful team culture that has become famous in English international sport. He has introduced a whole range of measures to make all this happen, many of which have their roots in psychology. The team has to change shirts at halftime to concentrate minds afresh on the second half. The changing rooms at Twickenham have been revamped to an impressive standard. Woodward insists that if England is to compete with the best they must have the best facilities. The changing room walls are adorned with motivational slogans, while the entrance to the players' tunnel that leads on to the pitch features plaques commemorating famous England victories.

Woodward has also introduced the concept of 'teamship rules', which every single player, 'even if they are the rugby equivalent of Ronaldo', he quips, signs up to. If any team member did not sign up to the rules, he would not play. These rules are created by the team themselves and communicated by team representatives who liaise with management. Among other things the players have banned swearing and use of mobile phones in public, they insist that players who are dropped must congratulate their rivals, forbid disparaging each other in the media and pledge to ensure that work is fun. (Source: an article entitled 'Now for the Next World Cup' by Larissa Bannister and Trevor Merriden, published in *Human Resources* in January 2004.)

IDENTIFYING ORGANIZATIONAL VALUES

Organizational values show customers, employees and other stakeholders how that organization intends to operate on a daily basis. Values are a set of expectations we have of ourselves and of others. The values state what is important for the organization. This solid foundation is essential to keep things congruent during change.

A recent study carried out by Professor Curtis Verschoor of the University of Chicago and published in *Management Accounting* (Sept-Oct 2003) found that companies with a defined corporate commitment to ethical principles fare better financially than companies that do not make ethics a visible management component. Public shaming of Nike's manufacturing sweatshop conditions and 'slave wages' paid to overseas workers led to a 27 per cent drop in its share price earnings.

There are a number of ways in which values can be defined in an organization. Here is one that we have used effectively in a number of organizations.

Values sort exercise

Put the following words on pieces of card or produce them as a list. You can add your own words to the list if you wish.

Freedom	Standards
Energy	Quality
Motivation	Professionalism
Focus	Avoidance
Controlling	Success
Leadership	Efficiency
Fun	Blaming
Passion	Achieve goals
Long hours	Caring
Friendliness	Innovation
Approachability	Customer satisfaction
Satisfaction	Respect for authority
Best	Continuous improvement
Pride	Competitiveness
Empowerment	Fairness
Excitement	Team work
Selling	Support
Over-promising	Reliability
Courage	Favouritism
Trust	Individual development

Respect	Quality of life
Risk avoidance	Discrimination
Humour	Equal opportunities
Secrecy	Straight-talking
Happiness	Short-termism
Justice	Experience
Diversity	Commitment
The status quo	Openness
Truth	Accountability
Disorganization	Responsibility
Honesty	Accessibility
Integrity	Internal politics
Sincerity	Sustainability
Self-preservation	Learning
Excellence	Under- resourcing
The words are a mixture of positive and negatives.	

The values sort exercise can be undertaken individually, but it is then best followed up through discussion so that people have an opportunity to recognize the prevailing current values as well as desired values. The gap between the two should promote debate. One way of doing this throughout the whole organization is to facilitate focus groups that are representative of all departments and hierarchies. This ensures that the findings from the process are valid. We recommend small group discussions (with six people with one facilitator), so that everyone can participate. The focus group can be run in two parts.

Part 1 asks the group to pick out the values represented on the list or cards that reflect the organization today. Ask them to position the values under three headings (which appear on the recording sheets below):

- What the organization values most highly.
- What the organization values slightly.
- What the organization does not value at all.

Part 2 asks the group to pick out the values represented on the list or cards that reflect the organization as it should be. Again, ask them to position the values under the three headings given on the recording sheets.

Note: if time is short, ask the group to focus on question 1 only (what the organization values most highly) in both Parts 1 and 2.

PART 1: THE ORGANIZATION TODAY

Valued most highly	Valued slightly	Not valued at all

PART 2: THE ORGANIZATION AS IT SHOULD BE

What should be in each category below?

Valued most highly	Valued slightly	Not valued at all

When you analyse the results of the values sort exercise, you are able to distinguish between the 'espoused' values of the organization (such as values in the future) versus the actual values. The data will allow you to identify what the majority of people believe the values should be for their organization. It is advisable to check these values again with a larger group of employees before communicating them to the rest of the organization.

This process was used recently with one of our clients in the entertainment sector, where a group of employees identified values of the organization now as:

- under-resourcing;
- over-promising;
- disorganization;
- focus on the short-term;
- risk avoidance.

The values that they wanted the organization to have in the future were:

- customer focus;
- team work;
- integrity;
- recognition;
- professionalism.

They then defined these values in terms of what results people would see or hear (behaviours) and then communicated them through their management team to the rest of the company. These values have also been the foundation for the development of a competency framework. As a result of this work, a new performance management process has been introduced and training needs have been identified. The organization is now recruiting against their competency framework. Their value of customer focus has encouraged them to put much greater emphasis on understanding their customers' needs, both internal and external. This has led to changes in what they offer and how they offer that service to better meet their customer needs.

DEFINING BEHAVIOURS THAT DRIVE OUR VALUES

This section introduces a method of defining the behaviours that drive organizational values. Having identified the values, many organizations fail to help employees to be specific on how to bring the values to life through their actions.

TRANSLATING VALUES INTO BEHAVIOURS

Often values are simply published in organizations, pasted on the walls and that act alone is expected to change the culture. An all-pervasive organizational SQ is about bringing those values to life in everything that you do and touch in the organization. In order for that to happen, employees need to know how to translate the values into action. What do they actually mean when they answer the telephone to a customer, ask for help from colleagues and interact with other departments? If these guiding principles are in place they form a security and boundary for all involved in change.

Good practice suggests setting out a description of the behaviours that epitomize each value and that are relevant to all employees. In order to do this, our experience shows that it is best to, again, involve many people throughout the organization to generate the behaviours. We recently worked with a group of 16 people from a service organization. The group of participants represented all levels and functions of employees, both at head office and throughout the store network. For each value they brainstormed the behaviours that they individually believed they would demonstrate.

Next, each set of behaviours was prioritized by the group to arrive at between four and six that described each value and which were applicable to everyone. Each person from the group then took responsibility for gaining feedback from their peer groups about the relevance of the values. Having gained this feedback the values were then introduced at a one day conference of all employees. The values were then reinforced by incorporating them into the performance management system.

One organization we worked with has 'Enabling' as one of its values and it defines the enabling behaviours as:

- involving others in decision making, encouraging alternative opinions;
- enabling freedom of action through providing clarity on direction, boundaries and scope;
- sharing useful information and experience, helping others to make informed decisions;
- developing others' performance through providing a mixture of supportive and challenging feedback;
- encouraging others to show personal initiative, taking responsibility, and learning from their mistakes.

Another organization has 'Straight talking' as one of its values and defines this as:

- providing honest and direct feedback;
- communicating clearly and directly;
- challenging openly and appropriately.

Another organization has a value of 'Integrity', defined as follows.

- I treat others as I expect to be treated;
- I admit when I make a mistake and do not look to blame others;
- I take responsibility for my commitment to colleagues and customers.

HOW VALUES AND BEHAVIOURS CREATE A SENSE OF RESPONSIBILITY

An organization in the automobile industry used a participative process to arrive at its values and behaviours. The employees understand what the values mean, their performance is measured against values and behaviours through their performance management process and they are 'called' on these criteria by their colleagues if they are not meeting these standards. This process stimulates a culture of personal responsibility.

This business has recently gone through a merger, which has created a lot of change. The organization is still practising and is true to its values despite the changes in structure and personnel. All new personnel are taken through an induction process which highlights the importance of their values and behaviours so every member is clear from day one on the expectations of this company.

ASSESS YOUR ORGANIZATION'S VALUES

Complete this final set of questions to identify at what stage you are in identifying and engaging with your company values and what you as a leader now need to do to develop the SQ of your organization:

- What are the values of your organization?
- What are the behaviours that describe each value?
- How well do you personally model the values of your organization?
- How well do your team members model the values of the organization?
- How strong an understanding do you and your team have of what those values look like when they are being demonstrated?
- How do you tackle the behaviours in others that do not model the values?
- How have the values been incorporated into your performance management, recruitment, selection and succession planning processes?

These suggestions and examples of developing SQ in yourself and your organization during change are the foundations on which you can then build the other intelligences.

13

An introduction to political intelligence (PQ)

As the world business climate changes, so the rules of the competitive race are being rewritten. The effect is to make people and relationships more than ever the key to sustainable success. Only through deepened relationships with – and between – employees, customers, suppliers, investors and the community will companies anticipate, innovate and adapt fast enough, while maintaining public confidence.

Tomorrow's Company

One of the four key points on the change compass is PQ. Specifically this chapter considers:

- What is PQ?
- Why is it important during change?
- Reactions to change.
- A model of political awareness.

At the end of the chapter you will find a model to help you identify your own level of PQ. The subsequent chapters provide guidance on how you can increase your PQ.

DEFINING PQ

Politics has a poor reputation amongst the general public. Political intelligence in the context of change is not about parliamentary politics or elections, rather the focus is on politics at work.

All organizations are political entities. Although it is often not acknowledged or discussed openly, politics are largely endemic to every business. As many people do not respect politicians, politics is generally regarded as unhealthy, underhand and egocentric. Yet, as this chapter will demonstrate, PQ can have a positive impact during change.

PQ is about working with integrity towards the common good of the organization, rather than for personal gain. It is not about the abuse of personal power. In order to be politically intelligent individuals need to recognize the power bases and sources of influence that they possess as well as those others possess. Their negotiation skills need to be well developed.

People with high levels of PQ know who to influence in order to gain buy-in to change. They know when to do this and the best methods for gaining acceptance to change.

PQ as we define it involves:

- being aware of power bases;
- understanding sources of power;
- recognizing levers of influence during change;
- developing strategies for influence;
- gaining buy-in from stakeholders.

THE IMPORTANCE OF PQ DURING CHANGE

Politics are most apparent when change is mooted. Cassani, in her book *Go: An Airline Adventure*, describes her time leading the low cost airline Go, then part of British Airways, where she was closely aligned with her boss, Robert Ayling. When he left, the new Chief Executive took a different view of the low-cost subsidiary. Before long Barbara Cassani was isolated and unable to influence successfully key stakeholders. It was decided to sell the business and Cassani lost her job; she left feeling bitter and a victim of politics over what she saw as good business sense.

When David Henshaw took over as Chief Executive of Liverpool City Council in October 1999, he had his work cut out. The council was third from bottom of the local authority performance league table with only the London boroughs of Hackney and Lambeth deemed to provide poorer services to their residents. Not only that, but Liverpool also had the most expensive council tax in the country.

Henshaw's brief was to cut costs and bureaucracy, stabilize the council tax, and improve services and information for the local community and the council's staff. Henshaw set in motion a modernization process that saw the authority's eight directorates condensed down to five portfolios, a new executive team and 2,700 jobs shed – 10 per cent of its workforce. Henshaw's political intelligence gave him the skills to influence and negotiate this major change by gaining buy-in from vested interest involved. (Source: an article entitled 'A Dynamic Duo' by Dominique Hammond, published in _People Management_ on 21 March 2002.) Symptoms of negative politics at work include behaviours that demonstrate resistance to change such as:

- open opposition to change;
- behind closed door lobbying;
- blocking proposals through arguments and counter arguments;
- back-stabbing;
- blaming others;
- self-interest;
- covert alliance forming;
- denying that change is taking place;
- agreeing to change in word but not in action;
- unspoken resentment;
- lack of cooperation;
- building power bases;
- inward focus;
- deterioration in productivity;
- lack of motivation;
- poor morale;
- being 'economical with the truth'.

However, politics can have a positive impact during change. It can create:

- a shared understanding of the need for change;
- a common sense of purpose;
- acknowledgement of the difficulties of change;
- disagreement aired openly and seen as positive;
- debate sharpening the quality of decision making;
- recognition of winners and losers during change;
- understanding of vested interests – who will help and who will hinder during change;

- feedback and recognition of the impact of change;
- change agents who influence others positively to accept change;
- experimentation and testing;
- win–win outcomes.

TYPICAL REACTIONS DURING CHANGE

In order to recognize why negative politics occur during change, it is helpful to understand typical reactions to change. These are linked to the transition curve discussed in Chapter 8.

Think of a time when you have been involved in change, no matter how big or small. It could be moving home, a change at work, having your children going to school for the first time or leaving home, a change of partner or bereavement. Listed below are the seven phases of the transition curve and the symptoms that you may see in each. Tick those that you have personally experienced:

---

1. Shock

A sense of unreality and being overwhelmed.

What is happening?	☐
Numbness	☐
Is this really true?	☐
A bolt from the blue	☐
Disbelief	☐
A kick in the teeth	☐

2. Denial

Ignoring the change. Focusing on the past. Building up your defences to minimize the disruption. Denial can even result in a temporary increase in performance.

It will soon be over	☐
I don't believe this	☐
Apathy	☐
In the past we…	☐
If I bury my head in the sand it will go away	☐

---

3. Self-doubt
The reality of the change becoming apparent and causing uncertainty. A decrease in performance. Depression.

I'm sinking rather than swimming ☐

I'm not sure what to do ☐

I can't sleep at night ☐

I feel angry ☐

I gave my all and now look what I get ☐

I don't feel like mixing with other people ☐

4. Acceptance
Letting go of the past and focusing more on the future. A willingness to consider experimenting with change. More optimistic.

I feel more hopeful about the future ☐

I can see where things went wrong in the past ☐

Maybe I could try … ☐

I want to take advantage of … ☐

OK, so I'm in this situation, I need to make the most of it ☐

5. Testing
Trying out new ways of doing things. Productivity starts to improve. Lots of activity and energy. Experimenting. Mistakes may occur.

I've so much to do ☐

I've lots of ideas ☐

I can't concentrate ☐

I'm frustrated that I can't get everything done ☐

I'm trying out new things ☐

6. Internalizing
Reflecting on why and how there was a change. Searching for the meaning of what happened and why.

Withdrawal from activity ☐

Quiet times, reflection ☐

Sharing of insights ☐

Talking it through with friends ☐

Searching for meaning ☐

---

7. Integration

Stability. High performance. Change has been thought through and new and better ways developed. Increased self-esteem.

Team work ☐

Confidence ☐

Clear focus and plan ☐

I'm happy with where I'm at ☐

The extent to which individuals experience each phase will be different. At the death of Princess Diana, there was public outpouring of grief, including shock, denial ('Was she really killed?') and uncertainty and self-doubt for some people, for example.

The length of time that people remain in each phase of transition is variable. Some people may be in denial during change while others are in the testing phase, for example. Some may never move to integration. Typically managers who are involved in creating change may be further on in the transition curve (see Figure 8.1) than their teams who are affected by change and may not yet be coming to terms with it. We have worked in many organizations who have encountered so much change that managers report becoming 'numb' towards it.

Organizational politics comes into play both in the descendant and ascendant parts of the curve. Why should this be so? People become unsure of their position, they may wish to protect their territory, they wish to influence others in certain directions, or scarce resources need to be acquired.

At the initial stages of shock, denial and self-doubt, the emotional climate of the organization will be highly charged. This can lead to 'huddling' into fragmented groups, complaining and blaming in a destructive way. Later on during changes some groups will start to benefit from change and some will perceive that they are losing out. Politics of influence will again be at the fore and new coalitions formed while old ones diminish. There will emerge the politics of winners and losers. The stages of acceptance and performance will lead to the establishment of regular processes for communication and settling differences. A more cooperative, orderly climate will often start to emerge.

A MODEL OF PQ

A model that helps us identify people's PQ uses animal metaphors. It was originally devised by Simon Baddeley and Kim James. It describes two components of PQ – ability to read the situation, which can be low or high; and integrity: people can be egocentric and seeking their own gain or unselfish and focused on the good of the organization.

There are four quadrants on the model that describe individuals' possible positions in relation to PQ. In the top left-hand quadrant are individuals who do have the ability to read the political situation – they know who to influence and how. Nevertheless they do this for their own self-interest. These are the wolves that have little integrity and are prepared to kill to survive. Sometimes hunting in packs, they can also operate alone – as a lone wolf. In the bottom left-hand quadrant are the asses. They, like the wolves, have low integrity and seek to further their own gain. However, unlike the wolves, their ability accurately to read the political situation is poor. They can make fools of themselves by trying to influence the wrong people, or influencing inappropriately.

In the bottom right-hand quadrant are the lambs. Their ability to read the political situation is low yet they have integrity and do want the best for the organization. Unfortunately, lambs can be herded, fleeced or slaughtered by wolves.

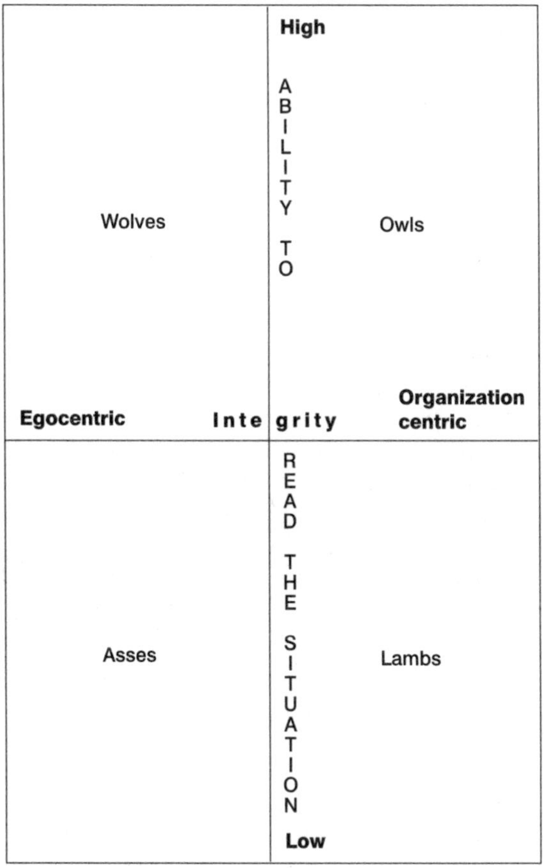

Figure 13.1 A model of political intelligence

In the top right-hand quadrant are the owls. Their ability to read the political situation is high and so is their integrity: they want the best for the organization. Wise owls, they are able to fly above the ground and see what is happening below.

Consider the organization in which you work and look at the model shown in Figure 13.1. Identify people who you consider to be:

- owls;
- wolves;
- lambs;
- asses.

Next, consider your own ability to read the political situation at work. Is this ability high or low? Are you aware of different stakeholders' needs? Do you know who to influence or are you largely ignorant of power bases and politics? Plot where you sit on the 'Ability to read the situation' axis.

Now consider your own level of integrity during change. Do you act for the good of the organization or are you interested in your own gain? Do you work for the good of all employees or are you more interested in getting the best for yourself? Plot where you sit on the 'Integrity' axis.

The key message from this model is the need to 'wise up' to organizational politics. Many people see themselves as lambs, not interested in politics and prepared to go with the crowd. Taking a 'neutral' or 'disinterested' stand is in itself a political statement. Therefore because we are part of the organization, we cannot help but be affected by politics.

The following chapters aim to help you increase your PQ. The intent is to be positive and helpful during change, to work for the good of the organization and its people.

14

Increasing your PQ

Having established that PQ is an important quality for change leaders, this chapter aims to increase your ability to read and manage the political situation with skill and integrity. Integrity is aligned closely to SQ (see Chapters 7 to 12). You will find some useful advice in developing your integrity in this section, too.

As a key component of PQ is correctly reading the situation, specifically this chapter focuses on:

- identifying stakeholders;
- taking account of the stance stakeholders may take during change;
- identifying driving and restraining forces during change;
- recognizing one's own and others' power bases.

IDENTIFYING STAKEHOLDERS

In any transition, change impacts people. These people who have a 'stake' and are affected by change, influence to a great extent the effective implementation of the change. The UK railway industry has undergone many changes in the past 30 years. From the 1990s privatization onwards, a series of radical changes has led many employees to feel disempowered. Many perceive themselves as victims of senior management and government decisions. One safety manager once told us 'I know there will be a big accident soon and I just can't get anybody to listen to put in place the right things. Management's priorities are elsewhere.' He was right; within the next few years there had been three major incidents with tragic loss of life.

In order to be politically aware, individuals need to openly recognize who will be affected by change, who are the winners and the losers, who may help the change process and who may hinder it. Having identified people's positions it is then possible to take action to influence others in a positive manner.

Stakeholder mapping

Stakeholder mapping is a useful technique that allows you to identify who will be instrumental in the success of change. The technique involves using a blank sheet of paper to brainstorm who will be impacted by change (see Figure 14.1). A useful tip is to break down large stakeholder groups into smaller discrete areas. So, for example instead of putting 'all employees' as a stakeholder, divide these into separate groups that may be affected.

Having brainstormed different stakeholder groups, the next phase is to identify who will be winners and who will be losers as a result of the change. (There may be groups that are not affected – they are neutral, or who may be both winners and losers.) Next, consider who will actively help the change and who will hinder it. Make a note of winners, losers, helpers and hinderers on the stakeholder map that you have drawn.

Figure 14.2 shows a stakeholder map undertaken by a manager who was responsible for relocating one organization to a site 5 miles away from the existing location and transferring the customer service department much further from the existing site – in this case, to Dundee.

A quick glance at this brainstormed map tells us that there will be some clear winners from the proposed move:

- customers;
- the executive board;
- the parent company;
- the future landlord.

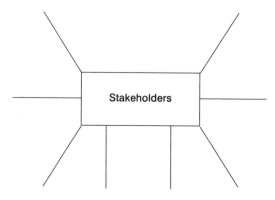

Figure 14.1 Blank stakeholder map

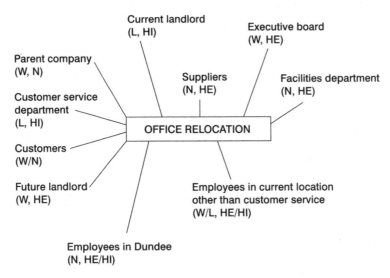

Figure 14.2 Stakeholder map for office relocation

It also identifies some losers, such as the current landlord and the current customer service department employees. In addition the map helps identify where there will be people who will help the change, such as the facilities department, and people who may potentially hinder the change, such as the current landlord of the premises and people in customer services who may decide not to transfer to Dundee. There are also some people that may be both helpers and hinderers depending on their personal circumstances, eg employees in the current location.

THE STAKEHOLDERS' STANCE

Having identified the stakeholders in change, the next step is to consider the stance that they may take towards the change. Consider the following questions to help identify possible approaches to the change:

- What happened during the last change?
- What lessons can you learn from this?
- How ready are people for change?

- What do they know about the proposed change?
- What has been discussed with them already?
- What have been their reactions so far?

It may be that you need to 'sound people out' about the change to gauge their likely position.

It is helpful to summarize each stakeholder group's stance towards change. Will they:

- be in favour of the change;
- want to keep the existing state;
- want to adopt another option.

Likewise it is useful to assess the degree of their likely response to the change, eg Will they:

- champion the change;
- be positive;
- be neutral;
- be negative;
- be antagonistic.

Figure 14.3 consists of a stakeholder template that allows you to summarize each stakeholder's position. It also asks you to assess their degree of influence and propose the action to take to enhance their views positively towards change. We will cover how to assess their degree of influence and how to influence positively in the next sections.

RECOGNIZING DRIVING FORCES AND RESTRAINING FORCES

A graphic way of understanding stakeholder issues is to plot the driving and restraining forces for change from individual stakeholders' perspectives. From an organizational perspective Lewin (1951) cites external driving forces that have a direct or indirect impact on the organization as typically being:

- changes in legislation;
- changes in competition and industry structure;
- changing customer needs.

On the other hand are internal change drivers such as:

- financial imperatives;

NAME	STAKEHOLDER GROUP	STANCE	VIEW	INFLUENCE	STRATEGY
List the names of the key stakeholders	List the group to which they belong	List whether their stance towards change will be: I = in favour K = Keep existing state O = Other opinion	List whether their view is: +2 Champions +1 Positive 0 Neutral −1 Negative −2 Antagonistic ? Don't know	What is their degree of influence: H = High M = Medium L = Low	Actions to reduce risks or enhance positive views

Figure 14.3 Stakeholder template

- the need to cut cost and improve efficiency;
- the need to increase customer and employee satisfaction.

Lewin and Senge (2001) describe restraining forces against change such as:

- keeping the status quo;
- fear of loss of power;
- fear of redundancy;
- fear of the unknown;
- lack of knowledge transfer;
- lack of time;
- lack of support.

Many of these driving and restraining forces could be seen to be present in the long drawn-out firefighters' dispute in England in 2003. A change in working practices was a precondition of a pay increase. The unions feared cuts, the employers were under pressure from the government to end cumbersome working practices and increase productivity.

A useful technique to employ when considering tactics for introducing change is to develop a force field analysis. This is a technique used to identify the forces that help or obstruct change. You can use this technique as follows.

1. Write a brief description of the change to be made.
2. List the 'driving forces' on the left (these are the activities that will assist change).
3. List the 'restraining forces' on the right (these are the activities that will obstruct change).
4. For each force, examine how easy it would be to change it and the impact of making the change.

Note: Reducing a restraining force is generally more effective than increasing a driving force.

INDIVIDUALS' DRIVE TO ACTION AND POSITIVITY

Robert Holden, founder of The Happiness Project, describes employees as suffering from change fatigue in an article entitled 'Look on the Sunny Side' by Sue Glover, published in *People Management* on 18 April 2002. 'People no longer clap and cheer new announcements. This has been replaced by cynicism about every new slogan and mission statement, which is largely a defence against old wounds. People are no longer excited by change; they're exhausted by it.'

Driving Forces $\rightarrow$	Restraining Forces $\leftarrow$
Training*	Staff shortages*
Process improvement	Call routing
Process maintenance	Additional tasks
Awareness	System performance*
Procedures	System defects
Instructions	Ignorance
	Unrealistic performance targets
	Boredom
	Commitment
	No time
	Uncontrolled changes

Actions denoted by *1. Review training of staff 2. Review processing equipment 3. Review staff shortages

Figure 14.4 Example of force field analysis

Imagine that you have called a team meeting. You are about to introduce a change in working practices to your team and you need the team's buy-in to make this work. This is the first meeting at which you have decided to introduce the idea. Take a few minutes to consider the likely reactions of your team.

It is likely that you have one or two people who will tell you why the change will not work, you have tried this before. These people openly block change. You may have some people in the team who do not say anything in response but you can tell from their body language that they do not think it is a good idea. Others, who are positive, make suggestions and volunteer to get actively involved. There may be several who nod in agreement and say they would love to help, but they have got a lot on at the moment. In order to assess the influence that individuals have during change, the change navigator can observe two sets of behaviours demonstrated by individuals. These are: their attitude towards change, be it positive or negative and their drive towards activity, be it inactive or active.

The degree to which people demonstrate a positive attitude and their type and levels of activity can be translated into likely reactions to change. The following model illustrates simple behavioural patterns that can be seen in people during times of change.

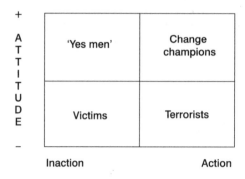

Figure 14.5 Drive to action and positivity

Change champions

They have a positive attitude to change and are action oriented. They are prepared to 'give it a go' and are realistic about obstacles they encounter and how to overcome these. Change champions react to change by:

- seeing the silver lining hidden beneath the dark clouds;
- viewing change as challenge and opportunity;
- treating life as a continuous learning experience;
- expanding their personal comfort zone.

Change champions tend to:

- feel comfortable with the need for change;
- be open to possibilities and ideas;
- be optimistic about the long-term future;
- like to be challenged and stretched;
- be realists, not afraid of short-term mistakes or setbacks.

Terrorists

They display a negative attitude and high levels of activity. These people are vocal but what they focus on is the negative. They are keen to disassociate themselves from change and actively tell others why it will not work. Terrorists react to change by:

- arguing against changes;
- always seeing the negatives;
- criticizing ideas and solutions;
- expressing frustration;

- focusing on the past – 'We tried this five years ago';
- being oblivious to the consequences of their negativity;
- bringing the 'victims' and the 'yes men' around to their perspective.

Terrorists feel:

- rebellious, determined to block change they do not own;
- 'right' and angry at the world for ignoring them;
- frustrated when there is confusion and 'whinging';
- not listened to, excluded, constrained;
- overtly confident in their own ability;
- unsympathetic to the stress felt by others.

'Yes men'

These people (men or women) are characterized by being positive towards change but not following this through with action. They say the right things and agree to change in principle but are inactive when it comes to actually doing something about it.

'Yes men' react to change by:

- acknowledging good ideas but being reluctant to change themselves;
- avoiding taking risks;
- keeping a low profile;
- trying to ride things out until things return to normal.

During change 'Yes men' feel:

- positive about what is happening;
- reluctant to get involved;
- threatened when too exposed;
- reluctant to take risks;
- comfortable to watch from the sidelines;
- anxious and lacking in confidence.

Victims

This group can be described as having a negative attitude towards change and lacking drive. This inactivity, coupled with their negative approach towards new ideas, leads to inertia. Although less vocal than terrorists, they still disengage from change, everything is 'done to them', they do not take an active part. During change victims:

- feel unhappy and/or depressed;
- feel overwhelmed by work;
- feel powerless;
- are fearful of mistakes;
- lack confidence.

Figure 14.6 contains typical phrases used by each type during change.

One argument (often put forward by terrorists) when we show this model is that we all move between quadrants, and demonstrate different behaviours at different times. Our experience is that under pressure and with the stress that change frequently brings, people tend to revert to a 'back-up' style. The back-up style characterizes reactions to change. So whereas in normal 'business as usual' situations people may be positive and have drive to get things done, during change their back-up style may reveal very different attitudes and behaviours.

Take a few minutes to look back at the model and the characteristics of each type.

Identify your back-up style during the last change that you experienced at work. Answer the following questions:

- What does this tell you about yourself during change?
- What reasons could there be for you to act in this way?
- Think about an occasion when you demonstrated this style. What was the effect on the customer, your team or your colleagues?

Now consider people on your team and their reactions to a recent change. What was each team member's back-up style during change? Plot the names on the model.

The next chapter discusses how to deal with people who are terrorists, victims and 'yes men' during change and how to motivate change champions.

	Inaction	Action
+ A T T I T U D E	'Yes men' *'I would'* *'I could'*	Change champions *'I will'* *'I can'*
	Victims *'I won't'* *'I can't'*	Terrorists *'It won't'* *'It can't'*
−		

Figure 14.6 Characteristic phrases

RECOGNIZING YOUR OWN AND OTHERS' POWER BASES

As well as recognizing likely stances and reactions to change, in order to influence change effectively change navigators need also to recognize and appreciate the sources of their own and others' power. Robbins (2001) viewed power as 'a capacity of one individual to influence the behaviour of another individual so that the latter individual acts in accordance with the wishes of the former'. Change terrorists, for example, hold power in a group as they strongly voice their opposition to change and play on fears to influence others to adopt the same view. Again, not overt, the extent of people's power bases has a considerable influence during change.

An organization we know had difficulty in implementing a culture change programme. The chief executive and his fellow directors had agreed to the programme and were instrumental in its design. Although not openly acknowledged, in reality there was an 'inner cabinet' within the team on whom the chief executive drew for support. Members of the inner cabinet were uncomfortable with the change programme and influenced the chief executive accordingly.

French and Raven (1968) identified five bases of power, namely:

- reward power;
- coercive power;
- legitimate power;
- expert power;
- referent power.

In 2000 Carlson, Carlson and Wadsworth recognized an additional power base: information power. Figure 14.7 gives a short description of each of the recognized power bases.

A person's ability to influence is attributable to the manner in which they influence (see Chapter 15) as well as the unspoken sources of power.

ASSESSING YOUR OWN AND OTHERS' POWER BASE

It is important from the start that you are aware of your own power base. We have worked with change agents in companies whose power base was low and unless they have increased their power they have subsequently found it difficult to influence effectively and change has suffered accordingly.

Look at the descriptions shown in Figure 14.7 and consider the degree of power you exert over others in each of the six areas. Rate yourself on a scale of 1 = low to 10 = high.

In which areas have you strong bases of power? Are there any areas where you could increase your power base to help you influence more effectively?

Reward power	The ability to influence behaviour by positive reinforcement and reward. Examples of this are praise, compliments and flattery, high pay increases, promotions, other forms of financial incentives, the ability to arrange desirable assignments and provide social recognition.
Coercive power	The use of threats and punishment to influence behaviour. For example threat of loss of job or demotion.
Legitimate power	This is power derived solely from one's position or job within the organization. Typically the higher one is in the organization, the greater one's legitimate power.
Expert power	This power base is used when other people are dependent upon one person for expert advice. This revolves around a person's technical knowledge and credibility (perceived or otherwise)
Referent power	Also known as 'attractive power' or 'charisma', this behaviour is characterized by people being influenced by the high regard in which they hold the personal qualities of the influencer. The latter is well liked and others see him or her as a role model to emulate irrespective of the person's status in the organization.
Information power	Access to information and the knowledge gained by possessing it is a further form of power.
Reward power	1 2 3 4 5 6 7 8 9 10
Coercive power	1 2 3 4 5 6 7 8 9 10
Legitimate power	1 2 3 4 5 6 7 8 9 10
Expert power	1 2 3 4 5 6 7 8 9 10
Referent power	1 2 3 4 5 6 7 8 9 10
Information power	1 2 3 4 5 6 7 8 9 10

Figure 14.7 Power base assessment

For example, referent power (role modelling) is an important source of influence during change (see Chapter 16) rather than coercive power.

Now consider someone whom you need to influence to change. Undertake the same assessment process (on a scale of 1 = low to 10 = high) for them. Understanding power and its sources gives us insight into how best to influence. For example, a chief executive with whom we worked scored highly on having legitimate, reward and information power bases. Realization of this helped us devise strategies to ensure successful management of the company's change process. He was able to be the centre of key information in change, which he publicized throughout the business through progress meetings. He was also very visible in the company, holding regular success meetings which recognized and rewarded key behaviours in customer service.

The next chapter covers strategies to use our power for influencing others.

15

Influencing others during change

Having identified stakeholders during change, their possible reactions to the change and recognized sources of power, this chapter focuses on:

- different influencing styles and their consequences;
- how to increase the effectiveness of your personal influence style.

INTENTION VERSUS IMPACT

When it comes to influencing others, on occasions it becomes apparent, either through receiving feedback or seeing for ourselves the result of our behaviour, that we have not had the impact we intended.

One Democratic candidate in the United States learnt to his cost the mismatch between intention and impact. During a televised debate he intended to speak passionately about his beliefs. Instead he was viewed by his audience as hectoring and verbose. His ratings in the polls subsequently fell.

When we do not influence as we intended, others may well not just stick to the facts of what we said. They are likely to refer to the type of words we used, the tone of our voice and our body language. This is an important component of the way in which we communicate. To have the impact we desire, our words, tone and body language need to be congruent and work in harmony. If our impact proves to be different from our intention, it is likely that our actions and words were mismatched thereby creating mixed messages to others.

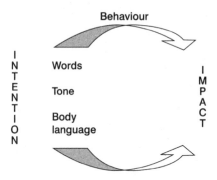

Figure 15.1 Intention versus impact

INFLUENCING STYLES

The impact that we create when we influence depends not only on whether our words, tone and body language are congruent, but also the degree to which we are open about what we need, want, expect, feel and how much consideration we show to others for their feelings, thoughts and opinions.

There are four main styles of influence that we can use with others, as shown in Figure 15. 2.

The most effective form of influencing style is assertiveness. Yet being assertive is not an easy choice. Instinctively when we face a threatening situation (as change can be), we adopt an emotional, approach which may be

OPENLY AGGRESSIVE BEHAVIOUR	People display a lot of openness but give little consideration to others' needs, thoughts or feelings. This behaviour may be described as domineering, pushy or self-centred.
PASSIVE-AGGRESSIVE BEHAVIOUR	People display little openness or consideration for others' rights. They find subtle ways to convey their thoughts or feelings to others. This behaviour is not direct and is often perceived as manipulative.
PASSIVE BEHAVIOUR	People display little or no concern for own needs or feelings in an attempt to satisfy the needs and feelings of others. This behaviour breeds low self-esteem, frustration and withdrawal.
ASSERTIVE BEHAVIOUR	People display openness and consideration for themselves and others. This behaviour allows individuals to communicate their thoughts and feelings in a way that does not violate the rights of others.

Figure 15.2 Influencing styles

	Openly aggressive Win Lose	Assertive Win Win
	Passive-aggressive Lose Lose	Passive Lose Win

High

D
I
R
E
C
T
N
E
S
S

Low

Concern for others

High

Figure 15.3 Influencing style model

fight or flight (aggressive or passive). Assertiveness is a rational approach based on choice and is a learned behaviour.

In order to influence assertively you need to be able to say what you feel and think and need while at the same time respecting and valuing the views and opinions of others. There are two sets of influence behaviours that individuals generally adopt at work as well as during change. These are called push behaviours and pull behaviours.

Push behaviours include:

- proposing – giving views and opinions, making proposals;
- directing – stating what you need and expect of others;
- evaluating – judging ideas and opinions given to you by others;
- incentivizing – providing incentives to do something or giving the consequences of not doing something.

People who use predominantly push behaviour work from their own agenda. They can be viewed by others as 'pushy' or aggressive. Their language is very much centred on 'I' – eg 'I want' 'I need'. The impact of their behaviour is that they signal that they want the other person to change.

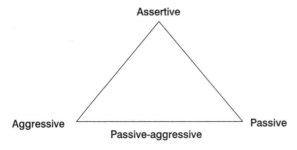

Figure 15.4 Assertiveness is a learned behaviour

The consequence of too much 'push' can be that people on the receiving end become disenfranchised. They do not consider that their opinions are sought or valued. In extreme a push style can appear dictatorial. The result of this style of behaviour is that team members lose respect for their leader and become terrorists (see Chapter 14 and below).

A further extension of push behaviour is manipulation – using sarcasm, withdrawing from dialogue with the other person, demonstrating through body language and/or tone that you are not happy. This is a form of passive aggression, sometimes called concealed aggression. The impact of this behaviour is that people become victims during change. Nothing is explicitly expressed, rather implied. An 'atmosphere' is created that is difficult to overcome.

Pull behaviours on the other hand focus more on the other person and involve:

- enquiring – asking questions to find out more from the person;

- listening and pacing – actively listening, summarizing. Matching the pace of the other person, going with their flow;

- being open to suggestions and ideas – being ready to admit mistakes, being open to other ways of doing things.

Rather than 'I', these behaviours focus on 'You' – the other person. They show an interest in and consideration for the individual. A further pull behaviour focuses on 'We': finding areas of agreement – building common ground, 'Yes, and ...' rather than 'Yes, but ...';

The impact of using a pull style of influence is to signal that you are prepared to change. You are working from the other person's agenda. However, if you adopt a predominantly pull style of influence all the time you may be perceived as 'a push over' or passive person. This style of influence can lead to 'yes men' behaviour in others. Everything is very cosy but no action gets carried through.

Tony Campbell, former Deputy Chief Executive of Asda and now non-executive director for a number of different companies, is quoted in an article entitled 'Board to death' by Jane Simms, published in *Director* in December 2003 as saying: 'I sometimes let rip on an issue and then have to rewind and reframe my comments in a way that elicits a thoughtful response. It's the difference between telling the executives how to do something, and helping them towards the right decision through persuasion and careful challenge.'

In order to influence effectively, therefore, change leaders need to adopt a style where both push and pull are given equal balance. It is particularly useful in conflict situations, with superiors or where you wish to gain buy-in, to use pull behaviours before push, eg use enquiry, listen and pace the other person. Equally in these situations it is important to be direct about one's own views and opinions, for example:

- 'What do you think about the proposed restructure?' (Pull question).
- 'So from what you're saying you believe ...' (Listening and pacing – pull technique).
- 'I agree that there has to be some leeway ....' (Finding areas of agreement – pull technique).
- 'The one area I need you to focus on is ..' (Directing – push technique).

The same principles of push and pull apply to the style of leadership you adopt in introducing change.

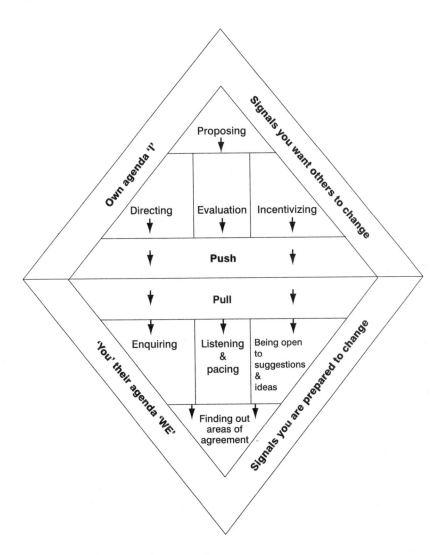

Figure 15.5 Influencing framework

An illuminating case study of a pull approach to culture change was the group-centred approach implemented by CEO Gerhard Schulmeyer in the mid-1990s at Siemens Nixdorf. By securing full understanding and freedom among employees of each stage in the strategy, Schulmeyer accomplished in one quarter what would normally take a year.

DEALING WITH CHANGE TERRORISTS, VICTIMS AND 'YES MEN'

As we have seen, the style of influence that you use has a direct impact on the reactions of others during change. If you identified earlier that you had terrorists, victims or 'yes men' on your team, here are some actions you can take based on push and pull to encourage them to become change champions.

Terrorists

Often people who have been with the organization some time and have 'been around the block', in order to become change champions terrorists need to:

- talk less and listen more;
- be aware of the negative impact they create;
- voice their concerns in a more positive manner and criticize less;
- ask to take on challenges and make the most of them.

As a leader during change initially adopt pull tactics with terrorists – ask them their views and opinions, get them involved. Give them responsibility for making something work rather than saying why it will not work.

'Yes men'

In order to be change champions, 'yes men' need to:

- avoid over-promising when they cannot deliver;
- if they cannot meet deadlines, enlist others' help;
- follow things through to completion;
- be more confident in putting forward and acting on ideas.

As a leader during change adopt push tactics with 'yes men' – set them targets and stretching goals. Monitor their progress and set them deadlines to ensure that things get done.

Victims

In order to be change champions victims need to:

- be more confident in themselves;
- ask for help if the task is too daunting;
- consider the impact they are having on others, play a more positive role in the team;
- consider what work they would really like to be doing, and do it.

It is probable that victims have worked for a leader in the past who has adopted a passive–aggressive approach. This style is one of an abdicator who has opted out of managing their team member.

In order to encourage victims to become change champions, start with a pull approach to find out what they like or dislike about their job, why they lack confidence. Move to push to set small challenges and to tell the people how you would like them to change their behaviour. Be prepared to have to have a lot of input with these people if you want them to continue in their current role.

Change champions

Do not forget to encourage and stretch the change champions. They too need a mixture of push and pull to help them to:

- set a positive example;
- put forward ideas for improvement;
- encourage and support their fellow team members;
- tell terrorists, 'yes men' and victims when they are having a negative impact.

WHICH STYLE OF INFLUENCE DO YOU USE MOST?

Answer the following questions to discover your own style of influence. Rate the following statements using a scale of 1 to 6 as follows:

1. Rarely do this.
2. Infrequently do this.
3. Sometimes do this.
4. Fairly often do this.
5. Frequently do this.
6. Always do this.

Please be honest! It is helpful to ask your team members, colleagues and boss to complete this questionnaire about you, too. This will help you to compare their impressions of your influencing style with your own.

Statement	Score
a) I put forward my views and opinions in a direct way	1 2 3 4 5 6
b) I make proposals with confidence	1 2 3 4 5 6
c) I state clearly what I need from others	1 2 3 4 5 6
d) I make my expectations known to others around me	1 2 3 4 5 6
e) I tell others directly what I think about their suggestions and ideas	1 2 3 4 5 6
f) I give feedback to others 'in the moment'	1 2 3 4 5 6
g) I give people incentives to complete a task	1 2 3 4 5 6
h) I tell people what will happen if they do not do something	1 2 3 4 5 6
i) I ask questions of others	1 2 3 4 5 6
j) I explore others' opinions by asking questions	1 2 3 4 5 6
k) I listen without interrupting others and summarize back what they have said	1 2 3 4 5 6
l) I match the pace of others in speech and body language in order to build rapport	1 2 3 4 5 6
m) I am open to new ways of doing things	1 2 3 4 5 6
n) I admit when I have made a mistake	1 2 3 4 5 6
o) I find areas of agreement with others	1 2 3 4 5 6
p) I build on what others have said rather than knocking them down	1 2 3 4 5 6

How to score

Total the scores for statements a) to h) .... These indicate push behaviours

Total the score for statements i) to p) .... These indicate pull behaviours

Now look at your scores for push and your scores for pull behaviours. In order to be an effective influencer, your scores should be within 3 points of each other. If one score is higher than the other by more than 3 points, this is the style that you feel most comfortable with. It is probable that you under-use the other style.

Think of occasions when it would be helpful to be more push or pull to influence others during change. Set yourself a goal of practising your under-used style.

16

Influence strategies during change

As we have seen in the last chapter, assertiveness is a key style of influence during change. The balance of push and pull behaviours, delivered in a congruent manner, help to promote a respectful and open environment. This chapter looks at:

- further strategies you can use to influence others during change;
- how to negotiate effectively;
- how to deal with difficult situations;
- managing conflict.

INFLUENCE STRATEGIES

In addition to the assertive techniques, in practice change leaders can use a variety of other techniques to influence others, such as:

- ingratiation;
- exchange of benefits;
- rationality;
- upwards appeal;
- coalitions;

- internal change agents;
- external consultants;
- physical changes, eg location;
- symbolic changes;
- sharing a common vision;
- role modelling.

Ingratiation

As the name implies, one method used to influence others is to ingratiate themselves via such approaches as flattery, compliments and providing support. The aim is to appear a loyal and invaluable person in the eyes of the person whom you wish to influence. In our opinion this is a passive aggressive-approach as it involves one individual is trying to manipulate another.

Exchange of benefits

Negotiating trade-offs is a tactic that some people use as a form of influence: 'I'll give you two people from my team to help you on the project if you provide me with the information I need from the report.' In extreme cases this can run as far as accepting gifts from suppliers, bribery and corruption.

Upwards appeal

If you are having difficulty convincing one person or getting him or her on your side, upwards appeal can be exercised by appealing to the person's boss or bosses. In this way you hope that the boss will influence the person to come round to your way of thinking. This tactic works in hierarchical organizations where you have a good relationship with the relevant boss.

Coalitions

Often used in organizations, forming coalitions involves aligning yourself with other people who share the same views as you. This tactic ensures that you will gain support from others in the face of opposition. Like upwards appeal, ingratiation and exchange of benefits, however, it can be a covert tactic and as such it can cause suspicion and mistrust.

Rationality

In this method the person trying to influence uses rational, logical arguments and facts to bring other people round to his or her point of view. An example of this is the use of competitive and market analysis in business to convince others of the need for change.

An advantage of this method is that people's readiness to change is a culmination of their dissatisfaction with the present state. Information that informs them of the problems with the present state can help increase and focus their dissatisfaction. However, it may not be enough to motivate change: positive images of a future state also need to be created to attract people towards a goal that has sufficient appeal so that they make the change happen.

Research shows that there are four hurdles to overcome when introducing change:

- the cognitive hurdle that may blind employees from seeing the necessity of change;

- the resource hurdle;

- the motivational hurdle that discourages and demoralizes staff;

- the political hurdle of internal and external resistance to change.

To break the status quo, employees must be face to face with the problem and appreciate why and how they must change. The New York Police Department (NYPD) in two short years transformed itself from the worst to the best police organization in the United States in the 1990s.

William Bratton, the department's Chief of Police, had to motivate 35,000 police officers to do an about-turn in virtually everything they did. To achieve this, he began to identify his key influencers. He targeted the 76 precinct heads who directly controlled between 200 and 400 police officers each. Getting these 76 heads galvanized to the new police strategy would have a natural ripple effect. The next step was to set up a very public 'fishbowl', a bi-weekly crime strategy review meeting that brought together the city's 'top brass' to review the performance of the 76 precincts, with all 76 commanders in attendance. As each precinct commander was questioned on decreases and increases in crime in their areas, enormous computer-generated overhead maps and charts were shown behind the commander illustrating performance of that precinct. The commander was responsible for explaining the maps, how officers were addressing the issues and why performance was going up or down.

These meetings instantly made results and responsibilities clear. The commanders who moved forward fast quickly became stars in the meetings, while those with poor performance were grilled and revealed before everyone. Within weeks an intense performance culture had been unlocked.

| Dissatisfaction | Attraction | Appeal |

Figure 16.1 Model of change (Dervitsiotis 1998)

When New York senior police officers were told to stop commuting to work in cars and to take the 'electric sewer' (the subway) instead, they immediately saw the horror that citizens were up against, with aggressive beggars, gangs of youths jumping turnstiles, jostling people and drunks sprawled on benches. With that ugly reality, the officers could no longer deny the urgent need for change in their policing methods. (Source: an article entitled 'Tipped for the Top' by Joy Persaud, published in _People Management_ on 24 July 2003).

Internal change agents

Many organizations select change champions to spearhead and promote change in certain areas. When Nationwide Building Society wanted to become a more customer-focused organization, it chose 12 people from different parts of the Society and at different levels to promote the culture change. They visited every branch and head office function to explain and discuss new customer-focused approaches. When healthcare provider BUPA introduced a new set of values and behaviours to the organization, it selected a group of senior managers to champion the change. These managers were well respected by their peers and team members alike and had 'bought in' to the change.

The advantages of internal change agents are that they can add credibility to a change project if they have the respect of their colleagues. The disadvantage is that on a personal basis many change agents find it difficult to integrate into business as usual once the change has taken place.

External consultants

External consultants can be used as an influence tactic to promote change. Often people from outside the organization and who are not part of the culture of the organization can make observations and bring objectivity to a situation. The difficulty in relying too heavily on consultants is the 'not invented here' syndrome. Employees can resent the influence that external consultants may apply. In addition there are sometimes difficulties unless the consultancy adopts a collaborative approach, in implementing changes once the consultants have left and in gaining genuine buy-in.

Physical changes

One radical way of influencing people's mindsets during change is physically to make changes to the location or environment in which people work. This tactic alone will not bring long term change in culture, but it can serve to heighten awareness of the change process. AXA Insurance, for example, tidied all their offices and placed posters and banners about their values from the ceilings and walls in an attempt to increase employees' awareness of the values.

Symbolic changes

Other organizations make symbolic change to indicate a state of transition and a change in the way things are done round here, for example:

- abolishing directors' parking;
- using first names;
- sitting senior managers with their teams, abolishing corridors of power.

If this is part of an overall change process, symbolic changes can have an effect but not if they are the only changes that occur. Supermarket chain Asda, now part of the Walmart group, ran a recognition scheme for head office where the winner had the opportunity to park for a week in the first spot right outside the front door.

Jobcentre Plus employs 35,000 people with Employment Service contracts and 55,000 from the Benefits Agency. When the new organization was officially launched in April 2003, the message to staff was that everyone should 'pull together'. The programme's change leader Saints admits, however, that this will be harder in the short term for staff still working in old-style offices. 'At a Jobcentre Plus, it's not just the décor but the whole climate that's different. It's far more professional and far more business focused.' What she is looking for essentially is a culture change. 'We are bringing together quite different cultures to create an organization with its own vision and values,' she says 'People change quite quickly when they see a different environment and behaviour.'

At a Jobcentre Plus, visitors are greeted by a 'floor walker' who briefly explains how the system works. Jobseekers first call a contact centre from the Jobcentre Plus and are given an appointment time (within four working days); they then return to meet a financial assessor (who explains the benefits they can claim) and a personal adviser (to discuss finding work). (Source: an article entitled 'Tipped for the Top' by Joy Persaud, published in *People Management* on 24 July 2003).

Sharing a common vision

An effective way of influencing others to change is to create a shared vision of the future. This needs to be sufficiently powerful to overcome the fear of the unknown so that the perceived benefits overcome the psychological costs. See also Chapter 12 for a process for creating an organizational vision.

Role modelling

Another important influence strategy during change is for key influencers in the organization to act as role models for the desired behaviours. Very often during change employees see their leaders do one thing and say another.

We have been involved in a number of behavioural leadership development programmes aimed at facilitating change of behaviour in the leadership population. Leaders gain a great deal of referent power when they epitomize in a positive manner 'the new way of doing things around here'.

How you act, what you personally say and do has great influence during change. Those people that are ego-centred and make all the decisions themselves do not role model a consultative leadership style. Do you role model best practice during change? Think of the last change that you were instrumental in driving at work, and then consider the following questions:

- Before the change did you consider the key stakeholders and what their reactions to the change may be?

- Before the change did you let your employees know what was happening in good time?

- Did you describe how you saw the change affecting individual employees and the workforce as a whole?

- Did you identify who would be most affected and consult with them first?

- Did you learn from past experience of change and let this influence your actions?

- Did you keep the amount of change planned to the minimum so you changed the most important things, one at a time?

- Did you think about the issues that the proposed change could bring about? Did you anticipate risks and any setbacks?

- Did you expect people to adapt immediately to the new work situation?

- Did you discuss each stage of the planned change and ask for suggestions?

- Did you anticipate the skills and knowledge that would be needed to master the change?

- Did you set a timetable and objectives so that you could measure your progress?

- Did you demonstrate flexibility in trying new things?

- Did you provide clear, accurate information to remind people why the change made sense?

- Did you hold one-to-one meetings, team meetings, use e-mail, intranet, newsletters, videotapes, general meetings, training sessions, posters, etc so that people received information fast?

- Did you arrange frequent meetings to seek and provide feedback and to have your hand on the pulse of what was happening?

- Did you provide more feedback than usual to ensure that people knew where they stood?

- Did you allow for resistance to change?
- Did you give people a chance to step back and look at what was going on?
- Did you allow for the withdrawal and return of people who offered resistance?
- Did you build bridges between your work team and others?
- Did you consider how employees were responding to the change?
- Did you recognize those who led the change?
- Did you publicly acknowledge those groups and individuals who have helped to make things happen?

ASSESS YOUR USE OF INFLUENCING STRATEGIES

Look at the list below and tick those strategies you have used in the past to influence others. Circle those tactics that it would be useful using in addition to assertiveness in the future.

	Used when	Possible use in the future
Assertiveness		
Ingratiation		
Exchange of benefits		
Rationality		
Upwards appeal		
Coalitions		
Internal change agents		
External consultants		
Physical changes		
Symbolic changes		
Sharing a common vision		
Role modelling		

NEGOTIATION SKILLS DURING CHANGE

There will undoubtedly be times during change when negotiation is called for. Karren Brady, the 'first lady of football' took up the role of Managing Director at Birmingham City football club in 1993 when she was 23. Since then she has turned round a run-down club by changing the philosophy of the business. 'The first rule of leadership success is: decide what you want and what you are willing to exchange for it' she states in an article entitled 'Changing Rooms' by Neil Merrick, published in _People Management_ on 16 May 2002. This is the fundamental principle of negotiation. This is particularly the case when decisions have been forced upon people and they feel they have not been consulted.

At Ford's Halewood plant in the UK, the senior management team drew up a transition agreement with the unions to enable the plant to operate the kind of flexible, Japanese practices common elsewhere, including Jaguar's other plants. In addition 500 jobs were to go, which strengthened resistance from a workforce that had already seen numbers drop from 13,000 at Halewood's peak to fewer than 4,000 by 1998. The senior management team produced a vision statement and negotiated the Halewood Gateway Agreement in which unions agreed flexibility, mobility and new working practices – including not eating in the cars. But when it was implemented, there was a series of protest strikes.

In response, Ford threatened to withdraw the project from Halewood, effectively closing it down unless workers signed up to a 'Halewood Charter' consenting to operating the agreement. Early retirement and redundancy were on offer to those who did not want to make the change, but there was a commitment to no compulsory redundancy. More than 90 per cent signed. (Source: an article entitled 'Top Gear' by Jane Pickard, published in _People Management_ on 18 April 2002.)

The longer resentment builds, the harder it is to negotiate. In 1984 Margaret Thatcher took a hard line with unions in the coal industry by announcing the closure of many mines. The Government's agenda was to increase efficiency and close uneconomic pits. The miners' agenda was to save their jobs and keep the pits open. There was no willingness on either side to give ground and what followed was a 12-month bitter strike. (As described in 'Top Gear' by Jane Pickard, _People Management_, 18 April 2002.)

When groups compete against each other certain behaviours prevail:

- The other group is seen as the enemy.

- Each group closes ranks and becomes more tightly knit.

- Each group believes that they are better than the other – they focus on their own strengths but deny their own weaknesses, while doing the opposite with the opposing party.

- As hostility increases there is a reluctance to interact with the other group.

- When interaction does take place it serves to reinforce stereotypes.
- The climate in the group becomes more formal and there is a focus on task.
- Leadership of the group becomes more autocratic.
- The need to present a 'united front' means that the group becomes highly structured and organized.

Many of these characteristics can also be seen in individuals who compete against each other during change.

Negotiation is a skill that is helpful during change. One change leader with whom we worked found his position weakened on the departure of his boss. The leader was responsible for the implementation of a multi-national change programme. In order to gain buy-in to the programme he needed to recognize the power bases within the organization and negotiate effectively with the key influencers.

To negotiate well requires mutual respect and an understanding of the principles of give and take. In true negotiations there are no winners or losers. The catholic priests in Columbia, during a time of great turbulence and change, managed to negotiate the freedom of many hostages from guerrilla troops. Individuals such as Kofi Annan at the United Nations are skilled negotiators.

In the Home Civil Service Sir Richard Wilson led a change programme to create a more dynamic and open service. After 18 years of government by one party it was recognized that the service did not have the right skills in place to meet the changing demands of customers and other stakeholders. Negotiating with employees and other stakeholders to find a way forward was key. A great deal of work was done around diversity and leadership. The emphasis was on team working rather than hierarchy.

STAGES OF NEGOTIATION

Geoff Armstrong, director-general of the Chartered Institute of Personnel and Development makes clear that 'Change was once negotiable but now it is inevitable and this puts different premiums on negotiation and bargaining skills – bargaining skills are now about being able to consult with both your unions and employees.' (Taken from an article entitled 'The Goals that Win the Game' by Karren Brady, published in *Director*, July 2003.)

There are six steps in negotiation:

1. Preparation.
2. Opening the discussion.
3. Stating objectives.

4. Testing issues.

5. Re-assessing.

6. Agreement.

1. Preparation

Most people do not spend sufficient time preparing for negotiation. During the preparation phase it is helpful to:

- Define the objectives. Be clear about exactly what you want from the negotiation and what you need to get to receive your needs. Decide what you are willing to concede in order to get what you want. Write down what you think the other party's objectives may be. What do they want to get and what could they give in return?

- Clarify the issues. What is the rationale behind your objectives? What is the supporting framework for your position? What is the best way to present this to the other party? What is likely to be the other party's position? How will they support this? What are the key differences between your position and the other party's?

- Gather information. It is essential to find out as much as possible about the person you will be negotiating with. What is his or her power base? What are his or her ego needs? What personal power do you have that can be used positively and constructively during the negotiation?

- Develop a strategy for achieving your and the other person's objectives. How will you conduct the negotiation? What is the best approach to take?

- Establish tactics for:
    - building relationships and setting the climate. How can you best establish rapport with the other person?
    - dealing with conflict: What will be the points of conflict? How will you deal with them?
    - resolution of issues: How will you attempt to resolve the conflict? What concessions are you prepared to make and when?
    - agreement: What should the agreement process be? Should this be formal or informal?

2. Opening the discussion

Your preparation will help you think through the best approach to take in opening the discussion. It is best to create a relaxed, informal atmosphere. Ask questions to find out more about the other person.

3. Stating objectives

Find out from the other person what he or she wants and needs from the outcome of the negotiation. State what you want and need.

4. Testing issues

Use hypothetical questions to assess what the other party is prepared to give and what they want in return. 'What ifs' and 'How would you feel if ...' are useful means of testing what concessions might be made.

5. Re-assessing

If there is a difference of viewpoint or disagreement, the best tactic is to:

- listen;
- ask questions;
- go back over the areas of agreement;
- take stock;
- restate your case;
- be creative – brainstorm possible strategies;
- solve problems jointly.

You may nevertheless encounter someone who will not give in. In which case avoid the impulse to lose your cool, but:

- persevere;
- listen;
- ask variations of questions;
- seek areas of agreement;
- explore alternatives.

6. Agreement

There are some simple rules about reaching agreement in a negotiation. If you are not sure, do not close the discussion. When you are sure, close. The temptation is to ignore important issues simply to reach the close. A useful tip is to try to reach agreement at each stage of the negotiation so that there are things you both agree to as you go along. Remember also to confirm the agreement.

CRITICAL MISTAKES IN NEGOTIATING CHANGE

Expert negotiators cite six critical mistakes which lead to stalemate or negotiations breaking down:

- **Lack of preparation**. Preparation allows you to consider what you need as well as the other party. It provides a good picture of your options and tactics.

- **Seeing negotiation as win or lose**. Each party needs to conclude the negotiation feeling that something has been gained. If you approach a negotiation thinking that you are going to 'win', confrontation is sure to ensue.

- **Use of aggressive behaviour**. Research shows that aggressive behaviour such as arguing, loss of temper and name calling leads to resistance in the other party. Assertiveness rather than aggression makes for a more effective outcome.

- **Talking too much**. People who talk too much in a negotiation do not create a cooperative atmosphere. Listening is a powerful way of finding out more about the other person's needs and concerns.

- **Ignoring conflict**. Conflict is bound to occur in negotiation. The temptation is to avoid the issues. However, in pushing them under the carpet you do not move closer to agreement.

- **Impatience**. Negotiations are often not concluded in one meeting. Ideas and proposals need time to gestate. A hurried agreement may mean that both parties do not get what they need.

DEALING WITH CONFLICT DURING CHANGE

People's attitude to conflict is rarely discussed. Many people back away from discord, wary of the problems it may cause. This reluctance may lead to avoidance of potential problem areas or suppression of disagreement. We recently worked with a customer service manager and her team to help confront the behaviour of two team members, whose clashes were having a negative impact on the customer service. Team members were, of course, aware of the problem, and had been for some time but no-one was willing to confront the issue in case they, too, became embroiled. However, denial does not mean that conflict goes away and it may get worse.

The other side to this is that some people relish conflict. The late Robert Maxwell was said to welcome a battle, haranguing people in meetings and threatening them. Some customers may deliberately adopt this stance in an attempt to get their own way.

Avoidance and aggression are not the only ways in which people react to conflict. Unassertive people give in and unwillingly collaborate with the other person. This may lead to an apparent resumption of normal working relationships but often at the expense of one person's self-esteem and a rather disengaged service team.

In many cases it pays to take a different stance and adopt a win–win approach trying to reach a compromise with the person. For example, a customer service manager may agree to take on additional administrative workload from another department if, in turn, the department is prepared to help the manager out when he or she is busy. By its very win–win nature compromise involves give and take. Research shows that few people adopt this collaborative approach to finding a solution, which fully satisfies the needs of both parties; it requires constructive building of common ground that starts off with thorough understanding on both sides. In our example is the customer service the best department to take over the administration? Why has the need arisen in the first place? When are there busy peaks in the department? Is the other department acting as back-up the best use of resource? What are the options? These searching questions can help form the basis of a lasting agreement.

Research backs up that more constructive and supportive behaviour towards customers and colleagues is a lot more effective than merely flatly stating obstacles and difficulties, which can drive people into corners they find difficult to back out of. And it leaves the problem unresolved.

PERSONALITY DIFFERENCES WITHIN THE TEAM

Lack of personal chemistry is one of the commonest explanations for strife; some people are simply incompatible, different as chalk and cheese. We have used two questionnaires, the Myers-Briggs Type Indicator® and Belbin Team Roles, very successfully to help people understand the positive aspects of the range of personalities and behaviours and therefore to view their colleagues in a new light. Different styles then stand a better chance of being appreciated rather than ridiculed or dismissed.

Note: MBTI® and Myers-Briggs Type Indicator® are registered trademarks of Consulting Psychologists Press Inc.

LACK OF INTERPERSONAL SKILLS

Poor interpersonal skills are a strong contributory factor in many disputes. We worked with one young, rapidly growing software house for several years on just this issue, emphasizing the importance of:

- listening skills, really hearing and understanding the other person's point of view;

- assertiveness, putting views over confidently and clearly;
- negotiation skills, reaching an agreement acceptable to both parties;
- handling meetings effectively;
- team working.

As one manager put it, 'The results have been beneficial all round. We still have internal differences, but now we talk about them and try to resolve the issues rather than harbour grudges. We have improved how well we listen and question our customers and really understand their concerns'.

ROLE CONFLICT, LACK OF CLEAR OBJECTIVES

In our experience a lot of conflict arises because of unclear definition and awareness of roles and responsibilities and a lack of shared understanding among employees of what they or the organization should be doing. Harvester Restaurants manage their outlets through self-managing teams. The teams regularly meet to clarify who is doing what and review progress against targets they have a hand in setting. This cohesiveness is positive for the customer.

POOR COMMUNICATION

When people are starved of information rumours start and mistrust can arise. Surveys have repeatedly shown managers pronouncing that communication is vital, yet being too busy to communicate effectively on a regular basis. Birmingham Midshires, part of Halifax plc, lays great stress on communicating regularly with employees to keep them informed of the business position and provide relevant information which affects them. The company conducts annual employee surveys to ensure that the methods used are effective.

CHANGE AND UNCERTAINTY

Change and uncertainty are a breeding ground for conflict to develop because well-established communications patterns are disrupted and stress levels are often high. In the 1990s Cigna UK undertook a large-scale business process re-engineering. As implementation proceeded it took a lot of time and trouble to understand reservations and difficulties expressed by employees and build modifications into its plans. Lastly it involved customers in the process; change implementation teams invited groups of customers to come in to see how the change was going to affect them.

LACK OF OPENNESS AND SHARED VALUES

The more secrets and taboos in a company, the more differences can smoulder without being addressed. One way to encourage greater openness is through 360° feedback, a method of all-round performance appraisal from colleagues, team members and even customers. Fedex is one of a growing number of companies who have used this method as part of a culture change strategy to build a more open climate where people can speak out. To promote commitment to a common set of values, healthcare provider BUPA agreed a set of leadership behaviours to encourage its managers to live its values. Managers throughout the business took part in a 360° feedback process, which allowed individuals to receive feedback from individuals across the organizations as to how well they were living the values. This was followed up by personal action plans.

STRATEGIES TO MANAGE CONFLICT EFFECTIVELY

Increase knowledge and skills in managing the conflict handling process

We believe everyone could benefit from better understanding of conflict resolution techniques. This especially applies to service employees, who are working in environments where they need to manage angry or complaining customers, either inside or outside the organization, and may often be undergoing a high degree of change. Here is the outline of the ground we might cover during a typical two-day conflict-handling workshop:

- sources of conflict between individuals;
- the consequences of conflict;
- judging peoples' reaction to conflict;
- conflict management strategies;
- skill and techniques;
- defusing anger and aggression;
- personal action plans.

Recognize everyone's talents

Jack Welch, when Chairman of General Electric said, 'GE maintains a huge trade surplus in talent. That's my job.' He actively promoted everyone's talents and contribution, careful to avoid the mistake of thinking everyone should be the same. An enemy of understanding others is the common assumption that the world should be the same as you, and if not then the other person or group is deficient or wrong!

Increase shared team understanding and values

Old style command and control businesses used to demand rigid conformity, which could lead to mindless uniformity and inappropriately sticking to rules. This is bad for ideas and bad for meeting individual customer needs.

To help promote understanding, sharing of common team aims and values are often used successfully. Team building needs experienced facilitation if it is not to degenerate into a false 'happy club' atmosphere or, conversely, one where friction gets out of hand. Equally, exercises to generate mission and values statements are meaningless if full involvement is not encouraged and actions and periodic reviews are not put in place.

All teams should be wary of the dangers of 'group think' and the 'Abilene Paradox'. This paradox was so-called because of the story where everyone in a family group on holiday went off to the small town of Abilene because no one spoke up, each person believing that he or she was the only dissenter. This story emphasizes the pitfalls of a complacent group where speaking your mind is discouraged. Our experience suggests that this danger is more common than is widely acknowledged in the excessive enthusiasm to create team spirit and harmony.

Recognize and address conflict

Conflict is a common occurrence in teams, particularly those that are newly formed or where new team members join an established group. 'Storming' is a recognized phase of team development. When conflict does occur, it is no use looking to others to take the lead.

If it is difficult for an individual team member to address conflict in their group, teams can usefully draw on the help of a coach or facilitator. This person acts as a neutral and independent observer whose role is to help the group achieve its objectives. One of the authors recently facilitated a team away day for a group of senior managers whose performance was felt to be lacklustre. The team had been formed nine months previously but had never taken the opportunity to review how it worked together. As the day progressed, it became clear that there were serious differences of opinion and clashes among team members. The facilitator helped the group to bring these issues to the surface in a non-threatening way. Although team members found the experience uncomfortable at the time, afterwards they reflected that it had been cathartic and helped them look towards more constructive ways of working together and starting to perform.

Clarify expectations

Clarifying expectations does much to ease tension where roles are hazy and misunderstandings build up ill-feeling. As a team exercise, we have used a simple format for team members to write down and then discuss one-to-one individual expectations with everyone in their team. We have used this exercise to develop a whole range of teams – newly formed project teams, established ones as well as with internal and external facing customer groups.

HANDLING CONFLICT IN SUMMARY

If we were to put advice into a nutshell we would pass on these tips to manage conflict:

- **Know yourself**. Understand how you typically respond to conflict. Practise being more flexible by putting yourself in the other person's shoes.
- **Listen**. Listen carefully to words and feelings.
- **Summarize**. Reflect back what someone said or felt to build greater respect and shared understanding.
- **Avoid tunnel vision**. Be clear on your case but do not become too fixated on your point of view.
- **Negotiate**. Be prepared to negotiate to reach an acceptable agreement.
- **Consider the effects on people**. Review the implications of major decisions on other people: it is easy to lose other people's involvement and commitment as you drive ahead.
- **Communicate**. Communicate regularly and build relationships, even (and especially) when damage has been caused.

DEVELOPING YOUR PQ THROUGH MENTORING AND COACHING

One way of increasing your conflict handling, negotiation and influencing skills is through mentoring and coaching. Executive mentoring has increased in popularity in recent years. Here a respected and experienced manager (sometimes external to the organization) is identified in the role of adviser, counsellor and sounding board to focus confidently on long- term personal and career issues. The mentee (senior manager) can draw on the wisdom and experience of his or her mentor to help him or her through difficulties and blockages. Our experience shows that many senior managers find the ability to confide in a trusted, external adviser an invaluable resource.

An international accountancy firm established a system of mentoring for its senior managers as a result of feedback from a cultural audit – employees felt that the top strata were out of touch and these individuals needed to change. Mentoring is particularly useful when the manager is new to the role or when internal politics prevent the manager from sharing personal experiences, for example in times of rapid and unpopular change.

Computer software giant Microsoft uses mentoring to allow people to re-centre and take a 'helicopter view'. The company believes that people need the time and space to share ideas with an impartial person. Mentoring provides this time and space.

Senior managers also are starting to be comfortable with using the services of coaches, either coaches externally resourced or trained by the training and development function, to help increase their immediate effectiveness. A coach works on a one-to-one basis to help the individual achieve his or her goals. Typically senior managers work with coaches to increase their personal performance. For example a French managing director of a well-known company was coached in persuasive presentation skills for presentations to his US bosses. The agenda for development if chosen by the manager can range from improving presentation skills to giving feedback, time management, organization and decision-making and influencing skills.

17

What is EQ and how can it help during change?

This section concentrates on EQ in relation to how it can help us during change. We will consider the following:

- What is EQ and how can it help during change?
- Assessing your EQ.
- What to do to increase EQ.

DEFINING EQ

To laugh often and much; to win the respect of intelligent people and the affection of children; to earn the appreciation of honest critics and endure the betrayal of false friends; to appreciate beauty, to find the best in others; to leave the world a little better; whether by a healthy child, a garden patch or a redeemed social condition; to know even one life has breathed easier because you have lived. This is the meaning of success.

Ralph Waldo Emerson

Emotional intelligence (EQ) is a phrase that has only become popular in the 1990s, yet this quotation shows that we have been aware of the power of it for many decades.

John Mayer and Peter Salovey in 1990 first coined the phrase 'emotional intelligence' (Mayer and Solovey, 1997). Since then Daniel Goleman has raised awareness of the nature of EQ and its influence on success in life. Starting with his first publication _Emotional Intelligence_ in 1995, he has been adamant that EQ has more to contribute to success than IQ and he has argued convincingly that high IQ does not correlate highly with success in the job. Goleman states that IQ contributes about only 20 per cent to the factors that govern success, while EQ accounts for the remaining 80 per cent. Undeniably, it helps to have brainpower, but this is not enough for success in leading change.

Emotions are the driving force behind all human behaviour. David Mead, Chief Operating Officer, First Direct says:

> For me the emotional side of the Customer Experience is the essence of First Direct. All the other things, the physical things, are what a customer is entitled to get from any bank. The emotional piece is what will make First Direct successful over the next ten years. For a customer to put the phone down, or click off the Internet and not only know that something has been sorted, but feel good about it means the customer would not want to go anywhere else.

Vice President of Marketing for IBM, Buck Rodgers said: 'People buy emotionally and then justify with logic'.

An example of the development of EQ at work is the way it has been instrumental in helping lawyers deal with emotionally charged situations. Following recommendations from the Macpherson report into the death of Stephen Lawrence, changes have been made in the way victims of crimes are informed about whether the case against their perpetrator will proceed to court or not. This was a role originally dealt with by the police. The Crown Prosecution Service (CPS) now has to contact victims of crime. They have direct dealings with them when they write or see them in person to tell them of the decision to prosecute. Over an 18-month period the CPS' 2,000 lawyers took part in a tailor-made training course based on EQ intelligence in order better to handle this difficult process. It was identified early on that given the rational, logical thinking style of lawyers, the change of role required them to think about how their decisions would make people feel and how best to deal with the subsequent potentially distressing discussions.

True _intelligence_ is having the capacity to balance information from the emotional side of the brain as well as the rational side of the brain and deal with that information appropriately.

THE DIFFERENCE BETWEEN THE EMOTIONAL AND RATIONAL BRAIN

The emotional brain is referred to by scientists as the limbic system. Why is it called the emotional brain? The limbic system stores all our memories from the moment we are born and helps us learn from past experiences. This therefore, provides us with our other way of 'knowing' – our intuition.

Intuition often becomes stronger as we get older because we have had more experiences. If we pay attention to this form of EQ, it can help guide our behaviour in a helpful way.

TUNING INTO EMOTIONAL INFORMATION

Our emotional responses travel faster than our rational thinking responses – it is the limbic system that warns us of an imminent crisis. Of course, as already mentioned, this is a plus when our safety and survival are at stake, but it clearly needs managing when the emotional response may not be appropriate in a work context. For example, your nervousness at an important meeting may have caused you not to 'think straight' and as a result you have been unable to get your words out!

The rational brain is called the cortex and this allows us to use thinking functions such as solving problems, making decisions, questioning information coming in, coming up with new ideas. The emotional brain and the rational brain are linked through millions of connections that allow each brain to influence the other so that information can be exchanged, analysed and acted upon.

In this book EQ is defined as the ability to understand and trust our own emotions as well as the capacity to read the emotions of others, so that appropriate action can be taken. In a later chapter you will have a chance to assess your EQ.

Many well-respected leaders rank highly on all dimensions of EQ. EQ is 'people-focused' and based on two major dimensions, intrapersonal and interpersonal competence. Figure 17.1 shows the EQ model we will employ.

The intrapersonal dimension focuses on self – self-knowledge, the personal approach, style and skills needed to manage self in any situation. The interpersonal dimension focuses on others – having a deep understanding of others' emotions and what makes them tick, finding ways to motivate them and maintaining harmonious and effective relationships. The following chapters look at each of these categories in turn and provide tactics for increasing your effectiveness in each area.

HOW EQ CAN HELP DURING CHANGE

EQ has risen to prominence as a response to significant changes in the working environment:

- The shift over the years from a manufacturing to a service sector focus has meant that there is a greater need for effective interpersonal skills. There is a need not just to engage minds but also hearts.

- There is a greater expectation from customers that they will be treated with empathy and understanding. Employees are customers too and they have the same expectations of how they will be treated internally.

INTRAPERSONAL	SELF-AWARENESS	SELF-CONFIDENCE	SELF-DISCIPLINE
	• Understanding and trusting your own feelings and preferences • Recognizing why you feel that way • Recognizing how your feelings impact on yourself and others	• Having belief in yourself • Being self-motivated • Having a style that is assertive and 'win–win' • Happy to make decisions alone and not dependent on others	• Dealing effectively with stressful situations • Managing your anger and impulse • Being flexible and adaptable • Creating a balance between rational and emotional considerations
INTERPERSONAL	EMPATHY	OPTIMISM	SOCIAL RESPONSIBILITY
	• Understanding the feelings of others • Putting yourself in the shoes of others • Picking up on what is being said, how it is being said and the body language that goes with it	• Taking the initiative, having a 'can do' approach • Having a happy disposition, seeing a glass that is 'half full not half empty' • Inspiring others by sharing what you are passionate about and encouraging others to do the same	• Putting others' needs first • Finding common ground with others • Minimizing conflict • Influencing others for the sake of the relationship or group

Figure 17.1 Emotional intelligence model

- The Service Profit Chain (created by W Earl Sasser, James L Heskett and Leonard A Schlesinger, 1997) explains that in order to get customer satisfaction and loyalty and therefore profitability, employees need to be satisfied and retained. One of the key ways of doing this is by showing them empathy, consideration and respect so that they become confident, developed and well-rounded individuals. This becomes particularly true in a competitive and changing marketplace.

- Shareholders are beginning to realize that it is not just hard, tangible facts and figures that create success and profitability in organizations but the significance of the leadership. The ability to lead and manage change in a competitive environment is critical to success.

- Change requires us to be more transformational in our approach to it than transactional.

- Stress levels have risen over the last decade due to the increase in the amount of change we are experiencing personally and professionally.

EQ AND TRANSFORMATIONAL CHANGE

Large-scale change generally requires managers to be more transformational in approach. Warner Burke (2002) and Warren Bennis (2003) have completed a lot of field work studying the implications of transactional versus transformational Leadership (see Figures 17.2 and 17.3). As the model states, we need to be more:

- innovative;
- adaptable;
- inspirational;
- speedy – (speedy means that we have to trust more in others, have a greater knowledge of others and how to get the best from them).

Day-to-day change too, now requires us to be less controlling and bureaucratic.

As leaders we need to develop our capacity to:

- 'let go' and allow others to take the initiative;
- trust our people more to make decisions;
- understand and involve our people at an emotional as well as rational level;
- be visionary, passionate and motivating in order to inspire our people;
- develop creativity and cross-functional working that is for the greater good of the whole;

- manage our own stress levels effectively;
- manage and be accepting of our own emotions as well as others' and the cause of those emotions;
- be more flexible in the approaches we take.

For this approach to be successful, EQ needs to be developed by team members as well as people managers. Team work across the organization is crucial. It means team members must possess the ability to:

- create social networks across the organization;
- discuss;
- interact;
- learn;
- collaborate;
- listen;
- share information;
- understand different perspectives;
- manage all kinds of emotions from self and others.

EQ AND WELL-BEING

Change often comes about as a direct result of an attempt to increase effectiveness. This can mean that each team member's responsibilities become heavier or more complex. Budget cuts are a common symptom of change that demands greater productivity from people in the organization.

With the increase in the amount of change comes an increase in reported stress levels and sickness in organizations. Research into this area conducted by Mark Slaski at Tesco showed that 36 per cent of managers reported feeling stressed, as opposed to 26 per cent of the total workforce (Wustemann, 2001). Slaski also learnt that long-term sickness numbers amongst managers were also rising. In his attempt to link stress levels, health and morale to EQ and performance in the workplace, Slaski asked a sample of managers to complete three assessments:

- The first was the general health questionnaire which assesses the individual's perception of their state of health.
- The second was an assessment using Tesco's critical success factor model.
- The third was the Bar-on Emotional Quotient Inventory which measures 15 components of EQ (the EQ-i). (Note: The Bar-On EQ-i is a trademark of Multi-Health Systems, Toronto, Canada).

The results showed that those who scored low on the EQ scored significantly higher on the poor health and well-being questions than those who scored higher on the EQ-i. Those with lower EQ ratings scored twice as high in the category of 'psychological distress'. They were also perceived by their managers as performing at a lower level than others.

Clearly, the implication is that the more we are able to increase our EQ, the more prepared and competent we will become in managing the changes that will inevitably arise in our personal and professional lives.

Bar-on EQ-i descriptions

The following sections describe the composites of the Bar-on EQ-i, which currently is the most validated measure of EQ in the marketplace. Individuals administering the test must be accredited in its use.

Intrapersonal

This area comprises:

- self-regard: the ability to look at and understand oneself, respect and accept oneself, accepting one's perceived positive and negative aspects as well as one's limitations and possibilities;
- emotional self-awareness: the ability to recognize and understand one's feelings and emotions, differentiate between them, know what caused them and why;
- assertiveness: the ability to express feelings, beliefs and thoughts and defend one's rights in a non-destructive way;
- independence; the ability to be self-reliant and self-directed in one's thinking and actions, and to be free of emotional dependency. People with high independence may ask for and consider the advice of others, but they rarely depend on others to make important decisions or do things for them;
- self-actualization; the ability to realize one's potential capacities and to strive to do that which one wants to do and enjoys doing.

Interpersonal

This area contains:

- empathy: the ability to be attentive to, to understand and to appreciate the feelings of others. It is being able to 'emotionally read' other people;
- social responsibility: the ability to demonstrate oneself as a cooperative, contributing and constructive member of one's social group;

- interpersonal relationships: the ability to establish and maintain mutually satisfying relationships that are characterized by intimacy and by giving and receiving affection.

Adaptability

Adaptability comprises:

- reality testing: the ability to assess the correspondence between what is experienced (the subjective) and what in reality exists (the objective);
- flexibility: the ability to adjust one's emotions, thoughts and behaviour to changing situations and conditions;
- problem solving: the ability to identify and define problems as well as to generate and implement potentially effective solutions.

Stress management

This category comprises stress tolerance: the ability to withstand adverse events and stressful situations without falling apart by actively and confidently coping with stress; and impulse control: the ability to resist or delay an impulse, drive, or temptation to act.

General mood

The two aspects of this category are optimism: the ability to look at the brighter side of life and to maintain a positive attitude even in the face of adversity; and happiness: the ability to feel satisfied with one's life, to enjoy oneself with others, and to have fun.

VARYING EFFECTIVENESS OF LEADERS DURING CHANGE

The Centre for Creative Leadership completed a recent study to discover whether specific elements of EQ were linked to actual behaviours associated with 'derailment' in organizations (Ruderman, Hannum and Leslie, 2003).

In the study, 302 managers and executives were rated in a 360° feedback process using their peers, bosses and direct reports. They were rated in terms of their likelihood to derail, destroy or damage a project or action. The five areas in which they were assessed were:

- difficulty with interpersonal relationships;
- difficulty building and leading a team;
- difficulty changing or adapting;
- failure to meet business objectives;
- having too narrow functional orientation.

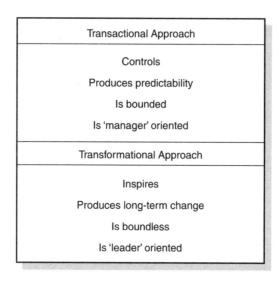

Transactional Approach
Controls
Produces predictability
Is bounded
Is 'manager' oriented

Transformational Approach
Inspires
Produces long-term change
Is boundless
Is 'leader' oriented

Figure 17.2 Transactional versus transformational approach to change

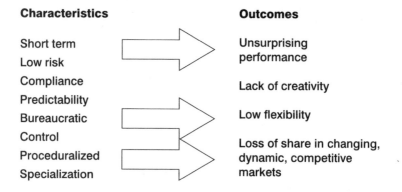

Characteristics

Short term
Low risk
Compliance
Predictability
Bureaucratic
Control
Proceduralized
Specialization

Outcomes

Unsurprising performance

Lack of creativity

Low flexibility

Loss of share in changing, dynamic, competitive markets

Figure 17.3 The implications of maintaining a transactional approach to change

The same managers also completed the Bar-on Emotional Quotient Inventory – EQ-i (a trademark of Multi-Health Systems, Toronto, Canada which assesses 15 components of EQ). The study found that certain aspects of EQ were moderately related to two of the reasons for derailment. The first was difficulty with interpersonal relationships. These managers were prone to displaying:

- insensitivity;
- arrogance;

- impatience;
- authoritarianism.

There was a relationship between this difficulty and the EQ-i scores on impulse control, stress tolerance, social responsibility and empathy.

The second aspect highlighted was difficulty with changing and adapting. This difficulty was also connected to low levels of stress tolerance and impulse control.

This study shows a clear need for competence in interpersonal relationships and the ability to change and adapt. Increasing EQ in these areas suggests that leaders will create a better outcome in times of change.

RELATIONSHIP BETWEEN CHANGE LEADERSHIP COMPETENCIES AND EQ

In 2001 Higgs and Rowland developed a set of leadership competencies that were associated with what was required to implement change successfully in organizations. Figure 17.4 lists these competencies.

Higgs and Rowland believed that there was a strong correlation between the change leadership competencies and EQ. They carried out a study with 70 managers and even though the sample was relatively small, their findings did indicate a strong overall relationship between change leadership and EQ.

CREATING THE CASE FOR CHANGE	Effectively engaging others in recognizing the business need for change
CREATING STRUCTURAL CHANGE	Ensuring that the change is based on depth of understanding of the issues and supported with a consistent set of tools and processes
ENGAGING OTHERS WITH THE CHANGE	Engaging others with the whole change process and building commitment
IMPLEMENTING AND SUSTAINING CHANGES	Developing effective plans and ensuring that good monitoring and review practices are developed
IMPLEMENTING AND SUSTAINING CHANGES	Developing effective plans and ensuring that good monitoring and review practices are developed
FACILITATING AND DEVELOPING CAPABILITY	Ensuring that people are challenged to find their own answers and that they are supported in doing this

Figure 17.4 Leadership competencies associated with successful change.

Activity

Look at the EQ model shown in Figure 17.5 and place a tick against the parts that you believe would be most critical to use or develop in relation to the five change leadership competencies. For example, if you think that 'recognizing how your feelings impact on yourself and others' is critical in order to create the case for change, place a tick in the corresponding box on Figure 17.5. Refer to Figure 17.4 to remind yourself of the definitions for the change leadership competencies.

Once you have completed this activity, identify where your top three **strengths** are in terms of the parts of the EQ model that you need to use and your ability to put those aspects into practice. Secondly, identify your top three **areas for development** in terms of the parts of the EQ model that you need to use and your ability to do so. Decide on some actions you will take to maintain your strengths and address your areas for development.

You will receive more help in this area in Chapter 19, which looks at how to increase your self-awareness.

Emotional Change Model		Creating the case for change	Creating structural change	Engaging others in change	Implementing & sustaining change	Facilitating & developing capability
INTRAPERSONAL	**SELF-AWARENESS**					
	Understanding and trusting your own feelings and preferences					
	Recognizing why you feel that way					
	Recognizing how your feelings impact on yourself and others					
	SELF-CONFIDENCE					
	Having belief in yourself					
	Being self-motivated					
	Having a style that is assertive and 'win–win'					
	Being happy to make decisions alone and not being dependent on others					
	SELF-DISCIPLINE					
	Dealing effectively with stressful situations					
	Managing your anger and impulse					
	Being flexible and adaptable					
	Creating a balance between rational and emotional considerations					

Figure 17.5 Emotional change model (*continued overleaf*)

Emotional Change Model		Creating the case for change	Creating structural change	Engaging others in change	Implementing & sustaining change	Facilitating & developing capability
INTERPERSONAL	**EMPATHY**					
	Understanding the feelings of others					
	Putting yourself in the shoes of others					
	Picking up what is being said, how it is being said and the body language that goes with it					
	OPTIMISM					
	Taking the initiative, having a 'can do' approach					
	Having a happy disposition, seeing a glass that is 'half full not half empty'					
	Inspiring others by sharing what you are passionate about and encouraging others to do the same					
	SOCIAL RESPONSIBILITY					
	Putting others' needs first					
	Finding common ground with others					
	Minimizing conflict					
	Influencing others for the sake of the relationship or group					

18

Assessing your EQ

In this chapter you will have an opportunity to:

- assess your EQ against the criteria described in the EQ model;
- identify where your strengths are, and areas for development;
- complete a diagnostic questionnaire.

The following diagnostic questionnaire will help you to assess your EQ and assesses the following areas:

- Intrapersonal:
  - self-awareness;
  - self-confidence;
  - self-discipline;

- Interpersonal;
  - empathy;
  - optimism;
  - social responsibility.

Rate yourself on a scale of 1 to 5 for each question:
1 = almost never through to 5 which = almost always.

1 When feeling a negative emotion (eg anger, sadness) I always consider the most appropriate way of dealing with this rather than allowing my negative emotions to take over.

2. I am able to motivate myself to achieve and deliver my goals.

3. I find positive ways of releasing my anger.

4. I am good at matching and pacing my feelings with the individual I am interacting with.

5. I can keep going despite obstacles being put in my way.

6. I act responsibly in situations even if it means I might not benefit personally.

7. When I am with others and my mood is not positive, I take conscious steps to change it to a more positive one.

8. I say if I do not agree with someone else's opinion.

9. I can deal calmly and thoughtfully with the emotional displays of others.

10. I find it easy to put myself in someone else's situation and understand what it feels like.

11. I see the bright side of things rather than the down side.

12. When there is potential conflict in a group I will search for areas of commonality and agreement.

13. When I display negative or positive emotions I am aware of the impact I am having on the people around me.

14. I show consideration and listen to other people's opinions.

15. I am able to be composed and control my aggression when something happens that upsets me.

16. I can pick up underlying messages from people through their tone and body language.

17. When I am enthusiastic or passionate about something I let it show.

18. I am accepting of everyone's talents and find effective ways of using those for the sake of the individual as well as the group.

19. I am aware of the circumstances or people that create positive or negative emotions in me.

20. I am happy to make decisions myself without having to refer to others.

21. I weigh up all the facts surrounding the situation before taking action.

22. I give my undivided attention to others when I am listening to them.

23. People often feel inspired or encouraged after having interacted with me.

24. I act as the conscience for any group I work with and when necessary, remind them of how we should be behaving with one another.
25. I am aware of the physical reactions I have when I am feeling strong positive or negative emotions.
26. I am respected and liked by others even if they do not agree with me.
27. I perceive myself to be flexible and adaptable.
28. People find it easy to talk to me about themselves.
29. When I see that something needs doing I go ahead and do it.
30. I find ways of giving my time to the community.

Please transfer your scores from the diagnostic onto the table below.
Add up each column and you will receive a score for each category:
SA stands for self-awareness
SC stands for self-confidence
SD stands for self-discipline
E stands for empathy
O stands for optimism
SR stands for social responsibility.

Q1	Q2	Q3	Q4	Q5	Q6
Q7	Q8	Q9	Q10	Q11	Q12
Q13	Q14	Q15	Q16	Q17	Q18
Q19	Q20	Q21	Q22	Q23	Q24
Q25	Q26	Q27	Q28	Q29	Q30
TOTAL FOR SA	TOTAL FOR SC	TOTAL FOR SD	TOTAL FOR E	TOTAL FOR O	TOTAL FOR SR

Interpreting your scores

If you have scored between 25 and 20 you have a high EQ score for that category so continue doing what you are doing. Scores between 19 and 14 represent an average EQ score for that category. This could be improved by following some of the tactics described below for increasing your EQ. Scores between 13 and 5 represent a low EQ score for that category. We strongly recommend that this could be improved by following some of the tactics described below for increasing your EQ.

Activity

Look at your scores for each of the categories of EQ assessment. Identify what your top three **strengths** are and what you will continue to do. Identify what your top three **areas for development** are and use the tactics that follow in the next chapter to form your development plan for improving your EQ.

19

How to increase your self-awareness

This chapter will cover self-awareness and practical activities for improving your self-awareness.

SELF-AWARENESS

Many would argue that self-awareness is a critical foundation of EQ because specific awareness is the first stage of change. If we cannot recognize how we are feeling, how we are behaving and the impact of these on others, then we are at risk of behaving in ways that will turn people off. Coping with ongoing change means we need to keep up with what we are feeling and experiencing at all times.

The Johari Window (Figure 19.1) is a model which can help us increase our self-awareness. It is named after the first names of its inventors, Joseph Luft and Harry Ingham. It uses two dimensions and two divisions of these dimensions to describe you: what is known by yourself, and what is unknown by yourself, and what is known by others and what is unknown to them. There are four windows that you and other people can look through. These windows can be big or small.

The Johari Window differentiates between our open areas and our hidden areas:

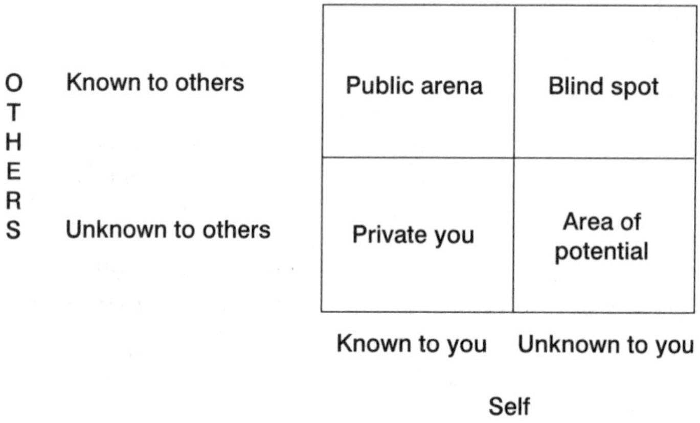

		Known to you	Unknown to you
O **T** **H** **E** **R** **S**	Known to others	Public arena	Blind spot
	Unknown to others	Private you	Area of potential

Known to you   Unknown to you

Self

Figure 19.1 Johari window

- The public arena is our public face – this is the window we choose to open in public. Here we find areas that we recognize in ourselves as well as what others see in us.

- The blind spot – sometimes people will see you differently from the way you see yourself and you may be unaware of this. Sometimes you may be displaying emotions or behaviour that is impacting negatively on the group around you, but you are unaware of that. Feedback illuminates the blind spots we all have about ourselves and increases our self-awareness.

- The private you – there are some things that you are aware of about yourself but which you wish to keep to yourself, particularly in a work context.

- The area of potential – this is the area of hidden, unknown potential. The aim must be to increase your self-awareness and reduce this hidden area.

The aim of the following activities or tactics is to reduce your hidden area of potential. Choose which you would like to complete in order to develop your self-awareness.

PRACTICAL ACTIVITIES FOR IMPROVING YOUR SELF-AWARENESS

1. Think of the image/perception you have of yourself and list the following on a sheet of paper:

- the first five or six words that spring to your mind;

- an animal;
- a musical instrument;
- a type of food.

The words you listed are indicators of your self-image. By interpreting what those words mean you will gain greater clarity of your self-image. Now:

- Interpret the meaning of those words.
- Note on a sheet of paper the elements of your self-image that you believe are in your open area (ie known to you and known to others).
- Note on another sheet of paper the elements of your self-image that you believe are in your hidden area (ie known to you but not known to others).

Each of us behaves in ways designed to allow various aspects of our self-image (known to self) to be known to others – an open area. Likewise, we behave in ways to keep various aspects of our self-image in our hidden area (not known to others).

Write down examples of how you communicate these important elements of your open area. For example, if you feel you are confident and believe that people see you as confident, what do you do to communicate confidence?

Write down examples of how you behave to keep elements of your self-image (known to self) in the hidden area. For example, if you feel insecure, but try to project an image of confidence, how do you behave to 'cover' your feelings of insecurity?

The second part of this activity will not just increase your self-awareness but would also be helpful if you needed to increase your empathy and understanding of others:

- Find someone who would also be willing to undertake this activity.
- Ask this partner to complete the activity on you while you complete it on him or her.
- When you have both finished, share your observations with each other.
- Identify elements that you thought were in your open area but were not known to your partner (ie they were in your hidden area).
- Identify elements that you thought were in your hidden area but were known to others (ie they were in your open area).
- Identify any perceptions from your partner that were blind spots for you (ie you didn't know about yourself).

2. When you next experience a strong positive or negative emotion, become aware of what is going on in your body physically:

- Identify any tensions or marked feelings in any part of your body, eg in your stomach, jaw, shoulders, etc.

- Release that physical tension using a few deep breaths or movement in the body to relax it.

- List the circumstances or people that seem to trigger the emotions causing these tensions and why.

- Examine the activities in the following pages to help you identify the best way of dealing with the emotions that cause tension.

3. Identify someone you value who will both support and challenge you. Then:

- Ask them for feedback about you as a leader.

- Ask them to complete the assessments in this book on you with specific examples to support their scoring.

- Ask them to complete a 360° feedback process if your organization works with this process already.

- Identify the top three strengths and areas for improvement that are most appropriate for you to increase your effectiveness as a change leader.

- Create an action plan to address these.

- Agree with the other person that you will complete this activity with each other every two months.

4. The purpose of this activity is to enable you to gain new insights and options involving situations which in the past left you feeling confused, fearful, stuck or frustrated. It allows you to communicate with important 'advisers' in your life, in order for you to create new alternatives for yourself in the future.

   It is useful to create Figure 19.2 on the floor and stand in the appropriate mapped out positions. The physical movement will help you with this exercise. Think of a current problem or situation which is causing difficulty or that you would like to change in some way and then:

- Describe it briefly standing at point A.

- Step to point B and bring to mind three people who you value, and/or have shaped and influenced your life in a positive way.

- Step to point C. Go into role as your first adviser, and describe the current situation or problem from his or her perspective. Speak in the first person, as if you were that adviser. What do you see/hear/feel? What insights and advice would you give about the current problem or situation?

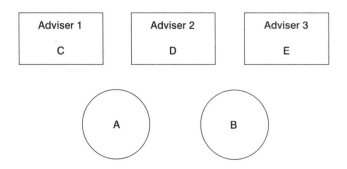

Figure 19.2 Self-awareness activity

- After the first adviser has finished, return to point B to check that the advice makes sense to you. If there is anything you do not understand from this perspective go back to point C and clarify.

- Step to point D. Take the role of your second adviser and describe the problem from this person's perspective. Speak in the first person, as if you were that adviser. What do you see/hear/feel? What insights and advice would you give about the current problem situation?

- After the second adviser has finished, return to point B to check that the advice makes sense to you. If there is anything you do not understand from this perspective go back to point D and clarify.

- Step to point E. Take the role of your third adviser and describe the problem from that person's perspective. Speak in the first person, as if you were that adviser. What do you see/hear/feel? What insights and advice would you give about the current problem situation?

- After the third adviser has finished, return to point B to check that the advice makes sense to you. If there is anything you do not understand from this perspective go back into point E and clarify.

- Once you have gathered clear information from all three advisers, go back to point B and identify the key themes and messages being communicated.

- When you have reflected on the common messages from your advisers, put yourself back into the actual problem you are experiencing by standing in point A and recalling it. Notice how your perception of the situation has changed.

- Use the messages from your advisers and imagine yourself in the problem situation in the future, notice the new options and resources that are available to you. Given that information, what are you going to do?

20

How to increase your self-confidence

This chapter will focus on self-confidence and practical activities for improving your self-confidence.

SELF-CONFIDENCE

Leaders who are able to display a positive, but realistic, attitude towards themselves without being arrogant will be well received by their people and will have greater success in leading change through their organization. Why? It is because:

- They are more likely to believe that they can achieve the desired outcome.

- They will be more willing to seek the views of others because they do not believe they have to have or could have the right answer all the time.

- They will be more willing to admit when things go wrong so there is an opportunity to fix things.

- The style they use will allow for consideration of others' viewpoints as well as an ability to express their own viewpoint.

- They will be more likely to take a risk and manage what comes out of it.

PRACTICAL ACTIVITIES FOR INCREASING YOUR SELF-CONFIDENCE

One of the reasons why we suffer from lack of confidence is because we allow too many negative thoughts to invade our minds, which in turn can create feelings of failure and rejection.

The first activity below will appeal to those of you who have a preference for auditory experience (ie you like to hear and listen to information). The second activity will appeal to those of you who have a preference for visual experience (ie you like to see and imagine the information).The third activity will appeal to those of you who have a preference for kinesthetic experience (ie you like to touch, feel the information).

1. Create a positive letter or affirmation for yourself.

- Write a list of positive statements about yourself that you know are true – at least six.

- Write them in the present tense using positive language. If you have completed the visioning exercise in Chapter 10 use that for added relevance. Examples might be:

    - 'I am a great leader of change who can make a difference';
    - 'I am a confident speaker';
    - 'I add enormous value to this team'.

- Keep these positive affirmations with you at work and read them out loud twice a day for approximately three weeks.

- After a time you should be able to memorize these so you can apply them during any stressful situation in order to alleviate your anxiety.

2. Visualize yourself being successful. The ability to see yourself doing things well programs the mind to put those steps into action – the mind cannot differentiate between fact and fiction!

- Think of an occasion or situation where you do not feel confident, eg giving a presentation in front of a certain group of people;

- Close your eyes and watch yourself doing what you want to happen as if it is on a video tape. Consider:

    - where you are;
    - who is in the audience or who is with you;
    - what you are saying and doing;
    - how you are looking – how you are dressed and presented;
    - the positive reactions from others to what you are saying and doing;
    - the way you are handling the group – your words, your tone and your body language.

- Play this tape over several times in your mind making the picture clearer and clearer each time.

- Notice the physiological changes you experience as you do this and how much more positive you feel about the event.

- Play it in your mind again just before the situation that you are not feeling confident about.

3. This activity is in two parts. Part 1 is a reflective activity to help you prepare for Part 2.

Part 1

Identify any individuals you feel less confident with. Choose one individual at a time and complete the following activity:

- Decide in what circumstances in particular you feel less confident with this individual, eg every time you interact with them, when you are at specific meetings.

- Identify what it is that the individual does or says that creates this lack of confidence in you.

- Identify what it is about how you perceive this individual that creates this lack of confidence in you.

- Identify what your feelings are on the occasions when you feel less confident with this individual.

- Identify how these feelings affect you physiologically.

- Identify what your words, tone and body language are like when you interact with the individual.

Part 2

Now refer to Figures 15.4 and 15.5, which appear in Chapter 15 on PQ, and answer the following questions:

- Using the information from Figures 15.4 and 15.5, decide how you would describe the influencing style that you use with this individual. Is it:
  - openly aggressive;
  - passive–aggressive;
  - passive;
  - assertive?

- Using the information from both Figures 15.4 and 15.5, decide how you would describe the influencing style that this individual uses with you. Is it:

- openly aggressive;
- passive–aggressive;
- passive;
- assertive?

- If you believe that the style you use with this individual is passive, you may need to use more of the push behaviours introduced in PQ to help you feel more confident and to be perceived as more confident by the other person.

Push behaviours include:

- proposing – giving views and opinions, making proposals;

- directing – stating what you need and expect of others;

- evaluating – judging ideas and opinions given to you by others;

- incentivizing – providing incentives to do something or the consequences of not doing something.

Some of your dialogue might sound like the following examples.

Proposing: 'Jean – I think we should consider the proposal from the Osprey Group as they have given us a great discount. I am free this afternoon, can we meet at 3 pm?'

Directing and incentivizing: 'Sally – I need us to reach a decision today about which supplier we are going to use. If we don't, we will miss the opportunity of putting it into next year's budget.'

Remember, you will want to match your tone and body language with the words.

If you believe the style you are using with this individual is aggressive or passive–aggressive, you may need to use more of the pull behaviours relating to PQ as this will help you get a more encouraging response from the other person. If the individual believes that you are willing to work to his or her agenda, he or she may change how he or she interacts with you.
Pull behaviours include:

- enquiring – asking questions to find out more from the other person;

- listening and pacing – actively listening, summarizing; matching the pace of the other person, going with their flow;

- being open to suggestions and ideas – being ready to admit mistakes, being open to other ways of doing things.

Some of your dialogue might sound like the following examples.

Enquiring: 'John, I heard you say you needed a Finance Status Report by 2 pm today, what would be the most helpful way for us to present the figures, given the few resources and tight deadline that we have?'

Being open to suggestions: 'Mike, I was thinking about your suggestion again today and it sounds like it may have more mileage than mine – are you free to talk about it this afternoon?'

If you believe the style you use with this individual is assertive, you may need to consider which of the push and pull behaviours you are currently using. Are you using the same type of behaviours all the time with the individual? Have you got a balance of push and pull?

Remember, if you are prone to using push behaviours all the time, it may come across as aggressive. Likewise, if you only use pull behaviours all the time you may come across as passive.

It is important when you want to be assertive that you select a balance of push and pull behaviours so that the recipient feels that you are indeed capable of putting your views across but you are also happy to consider and take into account the views of others. Practise your different styles and notice what happens to your relationship with the individual and how you feel about that person and yourself. Remember to modify your behaviour accordingly, eg if the other person is using a lot of push behaviours in one discussion, you should start with pull behaviours and then move into push behaviours.

4. During the next four weeks, at the end of each day, write down any occasions when you have behaved either assertively, aggressively or passively. For the times you behaved assertively write down:

- who it was with;
- what caused the interaction to be assertive rather than aggressive or passive;
- how you feel about yourself;
- how you feel about the individual concerned;
- what you will continue to do to remain assertive.

For the times you behaved aggressively write down:

- who it was with;
- what caused the interaction to be aggressive rather than assertive or passive;
- how you feel about yourself;
- how you feel about the individual concerned;
- what push and pull techniques you will practise to make this interaction more assertive if you are faced with the same circumstances again.

For the times you behaved passively write down:

- who it was with;
- what caused the interaction to be passive rather than assertive or aggressive;
- how you feel about yourself;
- how you feel about the individual concerned;
- what push and pull techniques you will practise to make this interaction more assertive if you are faced with the same circumstances again.

21

How to increase your self-discipline

This chapter will focus on self-discipline and practical activities for improving your self-discipline.

SELF-DISCIPLINE AND MANAGING YOUR EMOTIONS

Self-discipline allows you to display emotions that are relevant and helpful at the time and also to deal appropriately and positively with those emotions that would not be helpful to share at a particular time. This is crucial during change when all too often emotions created out of frustration are not always appropriate to share.

This does not mean that negative emotions should simply be bottled up. This would be a sure way to create stress and lack of self-discipline. It is about how and when you share those emotions with others and the way you choose to recognize them and then deal with them. Self-discipline means you can control anger as well as manage your frustration and impulse effectively.

Often in business people say, because of the amount of change going on: 'I just fly by the seat of my pants – I have to make snap decisions otherwise I wouldn't survive.' We are not suggesting that managing your impulses is about ignoring valuable intuitive, gut feelings but impulse control is about looking before you leap – knowing what information inside to listen to and knowing to think first rather than responding automatically. If you do not do this the decisions you make under pressure may be poor.

The inability to manage our impulses is often linked with an inability to manage anger. Anger, like other emotions, is neither good nor bad – how you respond to it determines the effect! If it manifests itself in rantings and ravings which create fear and paralysis, this will not be helpful to any group of people who are trying to engineer change as they will be fearful of making decisions and prone to hiding things which should not be hidden, for fear of further retribution.

We have been working with a company in the finance sector for the last few years. The company is owned by one of the biggest finance companies in the world. The division we were working with had asked us to work with them on their values and competencies and help embed this in the organization. The finance director of this company demonstrated an incredibly high IQ but he abused his power. He was also an extreme example of someone who displayed low EQ and in particular very low self-discipline. This manifested itself in the following ways:

- He actually screamed at people in meetings if they had not delivered what he wanted.

- He threw people out of his office if they questioned or challenged any of his ideas or decisions.

- He insulted people in public.

- He would ask someone to do something and when the person did what he wanted he would tell him or her that it was not what he wanted.

- He refused to become involved in any of the work we were doing with the organization and would withhold his people where possible.

What was the impact of this behaviour? Senior managers whom we coached would break down in tears because of the experience they had had with the finance director. Many of his senior team felt undermined, frightened to act and developed low self-esteem and self-confidence. He earned little respect and trust within his own team or among his peers. The change process was undermined at times by his behaviour.

Most importantly, the managing director chose to do nothing about the situation. What happened? The managing director was replaced by someone who possessed greater EQ and the finance director was replaced soon after his arrival. The finance department who were affected are regaining their self-confidence and have been instrumental in heading up a large change programme that has really turned the company around.

SELF-DISCIPLINE AND MANAGING YOUR STRESS LEVELS

To achieve self-discipline under stress you will need to have a series of strategies for coping with stressful situations, as well as an ability to stay calm and maintain control. The ability to remain relaxed when confronted with difficult situations rather than being swept away by strong negative emotions, is an indication of someone who deals well with stress. Poor control of stress can result in poor decision making and physical manifestations such as high blood pressure, heart problems, insomnia, panic attacks and weight problems.

Having strong self-discipline during change will allow you to manage your stress effectively, which in turn will help you to:

- gain a stronger sense of reality of the current state ;
- be more flexible in the way you approach your work;
- have greater impulse control.

Flexibility is a critical ability during change since leaders need to be able to modify their views when new evidence is presented. They need to be open to different approaches and be competent in handling multiple, shifting priorities. How does this differ from being impulsive? Being impulsive means that you make decisions without sufficient thought rather than in response to new evidence.

PRACTICAL ACTIVITIES FOR INCREASING YOUR SELF-DISCIPLINE

1. Reframing a situation can help create more desirable emotional states. This requires us to challenge the thoughts or 'self talk' that stimulate our negative thinking thus creating frustration or anger or negative moods.

    Think of three situations recently that have created anxiety, anger or frustration for you. For each situation ask yourself the following questions:

- How am I better off as a result of this situation?
- How might it have helped the other person?
- How might others have benefited from this?
- What have I learnt as a result of this not working?
- What have I learnt from going through this difficult time?
- How have I become a more enriched person as a result of this?

Repeat this exercise as soon as possible after the next situation that causes you to have negative emotional states.

2. Use this exercise to release your mind of physical tension or unnecessary thoughts. Have a clock in front of you. Now:

- Sit upright in a comfortable chair, unfold arms and legs and put your hands on your knees.

- Sit as still as you can for one minute.

- At the end of that minute, make a mental note of what you noticed was happening to your body at that time.

- Repeat the exercise for one minute, but this time, as well as sitting as still as you can, try not to allow any thoughts to enter your mind. It will help if you find a fixed spot ahead of you and focus on that or if you close your eyes imagine there is a central spot on your forehead that you are trying to focus on.

- At the end of the minute, consider if there were any thoughts entering your mind during that minute.

- Repeat the last activity once more trying your hardest to rid your mind of any invading thoughts.

If you practise this activity once in the morning and once in the evening, it will help to relax your mind and you will become effective at creating your own quiet space. You will then have the opportunity to fill this space with helpful, positive thoughts.

3. This exercise is a quick and easy way to feel instantly relaxed and is helpful if you are feeling stressed, angry, having difficulty creating a more positive state of mind or having difficulty sleeping.

- Choose some relaxing music to play in the background.

- Lie down on the floor, take off your shoes and release any tight clothing around your neck.

- Clench both fists as tightly as you can for a count of 10. Release and notice how much heavier they feel.

- Repeat this exercise with each of these other parts of your body: arms, facial muscles, shoulders, chest, back, stomach, buttocks, thighs, calves and feet. Remember to clench the muscles for a count of 10 and then release.

- Your body will feel heavier and you will notice a release of any tension.

- Lie still for as long as you can.

- Get up carefully as you may feel light-headed.

4. Identify the most common situations where you find it difficult to control your impulse or anger, eg during a project update meeting for the change programme you are involved in, confronting your least favourite client, etc. Rather than allowing these situations to control your moods, write down a plan of action regarding how you are going to deal with each one of these situations in a way that will have a positive outcome for you as well as the other people concerned.

5. This activity will help you to 'anchor' a resourceful and positive state that you can apply when you are confronted with one of the situations that results in a less than positive outcome for you.

Find yourself some space, peace and quiet.

- Identify a positive state or feeling that you have experienced in your life that you would like to be able to recreate quickly and have immediate access to it. This will be your anchor.

- Choose a signal that you can use when you want to access this feeling, eg pinching the flesh between the thumb and forefinger of your left hand or touching your little finger and thumb together on your right hand or saying a key word or phrase out loud.

- Think back to the time when the state or feeling you want to recreate was at its most intense. You must be able to see this experience through your own eyes – you must not be watching yourself in the picture.

- Step one step forward as if you are entering the situation:
  - What are you seeing? Is it clear, bright, fuzzy …?
  - What do you hear? Is it quiet or loud?
  - What does it feel like?

- Allow yourself to experience the feeling of being in the situation until that feeling becomes so intense that it envelopes you. As it reaches its full intensity, use your anchor, eg pinch the flesh between the thumb and forefinger of your left hand. Do this for as long as the intensity of the feeling lasts, then release.

- Jump up and down for a few seconds to release yourself from this.

- Repeat the process above at least three times until you can really feel the connection between the anchor and the state.

- In order to test the anchor, think of something else and then use your signal to anchor yourself.

- If the anchor has been released successfully you will see, hear and feel this state as if you were in it now. If you are not experiencing this keep practising the process.

- Now think of a situation in the future where you would like to have this anchored state. At the same time use the anchor and consider what you are now seeing, hearing and feeling. By doing this you will be transferring your resourceful state into a future situation.

- Use your anchor when this future situation arises and notice the effect. Any time in the future when you want to have this anchored state, use your anchor.

6. Think back over the last two weeks and identify any situations where you believe you were not as flexible as you could or should have been:

- What was the situation?
- What stopped you being more flexible?
- What was the impact of not being flexible?
- What could you have done to be more flexible?

The next time you find yourself being inflexible, consider what you could do that would show more flexibility and that would be acceptable for you to do.

22

How to increase your empathy

This chapter will focus on empathy and practical activities for improving your empathy.

EMPATHY

Empathy is the ability to tune into others' feelings. Without it we have great difficulty in maintaining relationships. During change, the ability accurately to read people's feelings is crucial, as potentially people will be in different places on the transition curve (see Chapter 8) and there will be a myriad of emotions to pick up on. The sooner you are able to identify these, the more likely you will be able to help individuals manage these emotions effectively, create an environment of trust and improve performance and productivity.

When people feel that you are on their wavelength, they are more likely to want to work with you rather than against you – exactly what you want in the midst of a change programme. A motor vehicle retailer we know was undergoing a lot of change with new products and increased volumes. This created difficulties between the managers in head office and the dealership managers. At meetings, the dealerships wanted to list all the things that the head office were failing to do and the customer problems that they were encountering because of head office. The head office managers wanted to list all the targets the dealerships had not met and what they needed to be doing to meet customer expectations more effectively.

As the amount of change increased, tension rose and the inability of the head office managers to tune into the dealerships' situation, and vice versa, dictated the customer experience and profitability. The only way forward was to facilitate a discussion which brought to the surface the reasons for the ill-feeling and how strongly each side felt about it. The next step was to coach them in the required skills to avoid this happening again. So what are the skills that you need to exercise in order to demonstrate empathy? They are:

- actively listening;
- reflecting back;
- summarizing;
- asking questions;
- paying attention to words, tone and body language.

- If you are able to demonstrate these skills it will send messages to people that you understand and are interested in their agenda. This is particularly useful in meetings when tempers are heated and everyone seems to be 'pushing' their ideas or approaches. Showing empathy at this time can create understanding between the parties and a quicker resolution.

PRACTICAL ACTIVITIES FOR INCREASING YOUR EMPATHY

1. Choose someone who you know is struggling with the changes that are happening in your workplace at the moment and work through the following structure, which uses the skills identified above as those required for showing empathy:

- Invite the individual to share with you any concerns he or she has about the change he or she is involved in.
- Give the individual your undivided attention and maintain eye contact.
- Listen intently to what the other person is telling you without allowing your rational mind to judge or evaluate the content of what he or she is saying.
- Match the other person's body language, tone and pace.
- Allow silence and nod to encourage the individual to continue (dialogue should consist roughly of the other person talking for 70 per cent of the time and you talking for 30 per cent).
- When the person has finished talking and there is a natural break, summarize or repeat back what the person said in his or her words, eg 'So it sounds from what you are saying that the biggest frustration you are having at the minute is getting the buy-in from the senior team?'

- In order to allow the individual the opportunity to be released from whatever unhelpful feelings he or she is experiencing at that time, try in your own way to feel what he or she might be feeling and make an observation about those feelings, eg 'I can understand why you might be feeling very agitated and frustrated by the whole experience'.

- Ask open questions so that you are showing the individual that you are keen to understand as much about the situation as possible and how he or she is feeling about it. Use open questions – eg How ...? What ...? Why ...? and When ...?

- At the end of the conversation make sure that you have asked a question to help the individual move forward: 'So what do you think you need to do to improve the situation?'

- Let the individual know that you are there as support when he or she needs it.

- Notice how this relationship develops and what improvements are made to the way this individual is able to handle his or her challenging situation.

2. Many of the most powerful activities to help you increase rapport and empathy are derived from neuro linguistic programming (NLP) which concentrates on modelling and defining what it is that other people do to be how they are. This activity is based on the work of Ian Ross from Vievolve, an organization specializing in NLP.

   This is a very powerful activity that will help you develop empathy with someone who you find difficult to have a constructive relationship with. Make sure you allow at least 30 minutes for this activity. You will need to identify a partner who can take you through each of the four parts of the activity so please make sure this partner has an understanding of the process.

- Identify a colleague with whom you do not have a constructive relationship.

- Identify a particular situation which you and this colleague are finding difficult to manage positively. Use this example to work through this activity.

- For the purposes of gaining clarity on which persona you should be adopting at any time, you will be referred to as 'John' and the colleague you are having difficulty with will be referred to as 'Peter' in the examples below. Please replace these with your correct names!

This activity requires you to assume three different perspectives or 'points':

- **Point A**. Being me – seeing the world through my own eyes, hearing what I hear and feeling what I feel – I speak in the first person, eg 'I hear him saying ...'.

- **Point B**. Experiencing the world as if I were someone else – putting someone else's head on! Sensing what the other person senses – seeing what the other person sees, hearing what he or she hears, feeling what he or she feels. I speak in the first person, eg 'I sense that the other person does not value my input ...'.

- **Point C**. Stepping outside and looking at the whole relationship as an observer. Now speaking in the third person, eg 'They are viewing things from different perspectives ...'.

Use Figure 22.1 to help you with the activity and place your chairs in the points indicated on the figure. The movement will help you to achieve focus for each part of the exercise.

Part 1

Point A. The partner who has agreed to lead you through this process will speak to you: '"John", imagine the person you are having difficulties with is sitting in the seat opposite you.' Now your partner asks you the following questions:

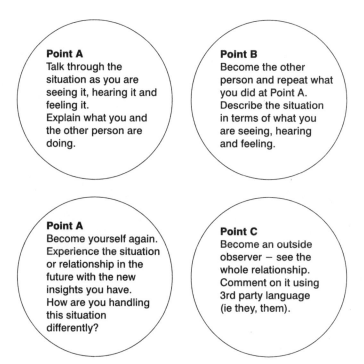

Point A
Talk through the situation as you are seeing it, hearing it and feeling it.
Explain what you and the other person are doing.

Point B
Become the other person and repeat what you did at Point A.
Describe the situation in terms of what you are seeing, hearing and feeling.

Point A
Become yourself again. Experience the situation or relationship in the future with the new insights you have. How are you handling this situation differently?

Point C
Become an outside observer – see the whole relationship. Comment on it using 3rd party language (ie they, them).

Figure 22.1 Empathy exercise

- 'What is the name of the person you are interacting with in your mind at the moment?'
- 'What are you seeing, hearing and feeling during your interaction with this person?'
- 'When you talk to this person what's your tone of voice like, where are you looking, how are you looking at this person?'
- 'What causes you to feel that way, to say those things, to use that tone of voice?'

Part 2
Point B. The partner who has agreed to lead you through this process will need to ensure that:

- you now move seats so you sit in the seat that your colleague ('Peter') was occupying;
- you adopt the body language, mannerisms, tone of voice of the person you are having difficulties with ('Peter');
- your partner uses the name 'Peter' when addressing and questioning you now.

Your partner will now ask you the following questions as if you are the person you are having difficulties with:

- '"Peter", when "John" is talking to you, how does he talk to you?'
- 'Think about his tone of voice – how does he sound?'
- 'When he talks to you, where does he look?'
- 'How does that make you feel?'

Part 3
Point C. The partner who has agreed to lead you through this process will need to ensure that:

- you are now taken to a spot in the room where you can see both chairs that you once occupied and your partner asks you to become an outside observer;
- you use the name of the colleague you are having difficulties with ('Peter') and your name ('John') – you do not use 'I';
- you talk about both parties.

Your partner will now ask you the following questions as if you are an outside observer looking in:

- 'Outside observer, what do you observe from out here about this relationship?'

- 'What are the dynamics of the relationship like?'

- 'Imagine that "Peter" is a metaphor for "John" to learn. If that were true what would the learning be for "John"?'

- 'If the metaphor were literally true would it explain everything that's going on in the relationship? If not, what does it not explain?'

- 'What advice would you give "John" if that were true?'

Part 4

Point A. The partner who has agreed to lead you through this process will need to ensure that you are sitting in the chair that you were sitting in when you 'were yourself' (ie at Point A).

Your partner will now ask you the following questions as if 'you are you' in Point A:

- '"John", as a result of those insights, what options have you got open to you now?'

- 'What can you do differently from this point onwards?'

- 'How can you improve this relationship?'

23

How to take a positive stance on change

This chapter will focus on optimism and practical activities for improving your optimism.

Throughout this book we have shown how to handle the ups and downs of change. Here we will assess your overall perspective and how it affects change. We will describe ways to retain a balanced and optimistic outlook.

OPTIMISM

Optimism is strongly linked with SQ, having the insight into who you are and what you stand for. Without a clear understanding of what you are about and an optimistic view of the future, your ability to lead change may be undermined.

We can differentiate between people who are predominantly pessimists, pragmatic optimists, and reckless optimists.

PESSIMISTS

These people:

- are likely to take a gloomy view of change and expect the worst;
- have an overwhelming feeling that 'failure' is permanent and bad things always happen to them;

- blame themselves for what has happened;
- believe that they will always be unlucky.

RECKLESS OPTIMISTS

These people:

- have an overly rosy view of change and its outcome;
- possess little sense of reality;
- function in a state of denial;
- refuse to be critical of themselves;
- believe that nothing is impossible regardless of the odds!

PRAGMATIC OPTIMISTS

These people:

- have the ability to look on the bright side of change in a grounded way and still be positive when they face drawbacks;
- regard change as an opportunity, but are not blind to possible problems;
- treat 'failure' and blockages as a temporary state;
- see one unsuccessful situation that has not worked out rather than one of many things that are creating a pattern of continuous failure;
- do not blame themselves for everything if there are outside forces playing a part in the outcome – they share responsibility.

People who are optimistic are often good to be with and are usually people with a real sense of passion. They are able to share what their passions are and breed a state of infection around them. People want to be with them.

The other area associated with optimism is happiness.

HAPPINESS

Happiness can be defined as general contentment in both work and leisure, combined with the ability to enjoy any opportunity to have fun. Those of us who experience more unhappiness than happiness may be reliant on our happiness being provided from an external source, eg winning the lottery! Stephen Covey, author of _Seven Habits of Highly Successful People_, believes real happiness comes from within and we achieve that through controlling our own lives by setting realistic, achievable goals that we want.

South West Airlines is a great example of a company who really know what they are about and stand out. By knowing this, their success has been due to the way they display their optimism, passion and happiness. Herb Kelleher, the President, CEO and Chairman of the Board from 1982 until 1999, described their brand as 'Fun and Family'. He demonstrated that in everything he did and his people did exactly the same.

How did Kelleher achieve this success in such a vulnerable, changing marketplace? His approach is based on the following:

- His passion about his business and his customers was his source of inspiration to himself and the people around him. He talks about South West Airlines always retaining a 'patina of spirituality' and cynics have often compared the company to some sort of religious cult, but employees and customers believe they are part of the South West Airlines family.

- His sense of fun and his need for fun is what made him and his company attractive.

- He has been referred to as the High Priest of Ha-Ha and has been seen in corporate videos dressed as Elvis and the Easter Bunny! He is not afraid to express his sense of fun – this is replicated on the aircraft between crew and customers.

- He has spent time around his people – it was not uncommon for him to drink with mechanics in a bar until the early hours of the morning to find out what was going on.

- His 'can-do' attitude and optimism shine through – the fact that he started the airline up in the first place shows his belief in himself and that anything can be accomplished.

- Kelleher says that he fears the absence of change. In the last recession before his retirement as CEO he released a cost-cutting memo warning about recession saying: 'When you think you've got it all figured out, then you're probably already heading downhill.'

How did this optimism impact on South West Airline's ability to cope with change?

- Despite the many recessions and economic downturns that have hit the airline business in the last 20 years (9/11 aside), Kelleher has shown optimism in the face of adversity and has continued to grow the business.

- His passion and happy disposition mean that employees are knowledgeable about their purpose and how they add value. This is why in a company where 90 per cent of the workforce is unionized, he can get cabin crew to perform both air and ground duties and make changes as required by customers or the business. It has allowed him to manage costs effectively.

- South West Airlines receives hundreds of thousands of applications for employment every year and takes approximately 3 per cent. They are able to get the crème de la crème who are recruited against a set of criteria that matches the company's culture.

- Because of the excellent workforce relationship, South West Airlines have the lowest number of employees per aircraft, the lowest cost per available set mile and the highest passengers per employee. This means that they can be very adaptable.

- South West Airlines has been the most profitable US airline for the last 30 years and the only profitable airline since 9/11.

(Source: South West Airlines' Web site, www.southwest.com)

PRACTICAL ACTIVITIES FOR INCREASING YOUR OPTIMISM

1. Identify what you are passionate about or what you love to do. If you have lost touch with what those things are, write down what you were passionate about in the past. Ask yourself which, if any, of those passions you would like to regain. Choose one and make a note of what action you will take to move it forward.

2. On your next 'away day' create some time to get to know your team better and for them to get to know you better. Present it as an opportunity to reflect and to talk about them.

Ask the team (include yourself in this) to bring with them something that inspires them. Check beforehand that all team members are willing to do this. In a relaxed atmosphere ask each team member to answer the following questions:

- What is your inspiration?
- Why did your example inspire you?
- What were the feelings you experienced when first inspired by your example?
- What was the emotional impact of your inspiration and as a result what did it cause you to do?
- How does your inspiration help you when you are coping with change?

After all inspirations have been aired ask the group:

- how many of them were inspired by others' inspirations;
- how has this helped them to understand each other and be inspired by each other more;
- how will they be able to replicate this understanding and appreciation in the workplace;

- how will this help them deal with the way they are managing change.

After the event record:

- what you learnt about your team members;
- what inspired you about them and what can you learn from that;
- what you did to inspire them and how you will continue to do that;
- how you can apply this inspiration during change.

3. Identify someone you know who you believe is very optimistic and get this person's permission for him or her to be your 'role model for optimism'. Observe the person when you can and write down or notice how he or she interacts with others, particularly details of:

- words the person uses;
- the person' s tone of voice ;
- his or her body language;
- the reaction the person creates in the people he or she is interacting with;
- what is different about the way you do and create all of the above;
- what you will try that is different.

Ask the person to describe roughly his or her 'self talk' (ie the things the person says to himself or herself) and immediate actions in the following situations – when he or she:

- first gets up in the morning;
- plans his or her day at the office;
- has something happen that he or she was not expecting;
- has to make a change to something;
- does not get what he or she wants;
- feels disappointed;
- has just been given some feedback from the boss on what he or she needs to do differently.

Following the activity:

- What have you noticed that is different about your 'self talk' and actions and those of your role model?
- What will you try as a result of this?
- How will this help you manage change more effectively?

4. This activity asks you to identify your level of happiness and asks you to consider how you could increase it if appropriate. Create a happiness scale where 1 = really unhappy and 10 = really happy. Position yourself on that scale. If you score your happiness at below 6 think about the following questions:

- What are the things you really enjoy doing?
- When did you last do any of those things?
- How frequently do you do them?
- Which of those things are you going to do more of?
- Who are the people you know who make you laugh most?
- When did you last see them?
- How could you see them more?
- When did you last do something spontaneous?
- How did it make you feel?

After answering these questions select one thing that you are going to put into practice next week.

24

How to increase socially responsible change

This chapter will focus on practical activities for improving your awareness and ability to be socially responsible. Change actions inevitably affect a wider sphere of society and have sometimes unintended consequences on people and the environment.

SOCIAL RESPONSIBILITY

Social responsibility means that you are able to contribute and cooperate constructively in the social groups you are involved in. It means that:

- you take responsibility for your behaviour and its impact on others;
- you are involved in activities which benefit others even though you may not directly benefit in return;
- you are aware that people who have strong social responsibility have a basic concern for others.

By helping others you often enhance the meaning of your own life. By focusing on others who have more serious problems and dilemmas, you may gain new perspectives on your own problems and dilemmas, whether that is colleague to colleague in an organization or involving the organization in relation to the outside world.

Boots has made great strides in corporate social responsibility (CSR). It was among the first to champion family-friendly policies for employees. In

2001, Boots became the first organization to offer staff formal accreditation for their work in the community. Voluntary work plays a large part in its CSR programme. The company started a Skills for Life scheme that offered employees the chance to be involved in community activities during company time. In 2002 Boots' employees spent 50,000 hours on voluntary activities, which equates to £500,000. (Source: an article entitled 'In Good Company' by Joy Persaud in *People Management*, published on 10 July 2003.)

We can look at social responsibility from the perspective of the individual in change as well as the organization and the community as a whole.

HOW SOCIAL RESPONSIBILITY HELPS DURING CHANGE

At an individual level, we would expect social responsibility to be exhibited in the way colleagues help each other in their teams, for example:

- A project team up against a tight deadline helps a vital team member who is suffering from family problems.

- Individuals and teams offer each other feedback constructively so that change projects stay on target.

- Individuals and teams reach agreement on common ground to move things forward, rather than wasting their effort lobbying and politicking to gain support for something that does not benefit the ultimate goal.

At an organizational level, we would expect social responsibility to be exhibited in the ways that companies help their local communities or charities. Take the example of the Co-operative Societies, which are in business for their members, not primarily for institutional shareholders. The Co-operative Movement started in Britain in 1844 in Rochdale, Lancashire when 28 pioneers set up a cooperatively run shop to counter the actions of exploitative factory managers and shop owners. Their values still centre on looking after the interests of the local and wider communities. Since 1992 the Co-operative Bank has adopted an ethical policy which recognizes the far-reaching and profound impact of its decisions, particularly in relation to its investments.

One of the Co-operatives that we have worked with published in their 'Vision and Values' booklet: 'Being a Co-operative means that we have differences from what others understand a company to be. We have shares but these are owned by members, not shareholders. Our activities have an additional purpose as well as financial success. We make a difference for our customers, members and people, not faceless investors.'

It is our personal view that one of the reasons why Co-operatives still retain their presence after all these years of major change is because their members have truly bought into what they stand for and continue to support them, sometimes even though they might not be the cheapest option or the best. Our observation is that their members can also be remarkably forgiving of the Co-operatives when they are trying to introduce painful changes.

Members encourage and support if they believe that the change is going to make a difference to them and to the longevity of the Society.

ACTIVITIES INVOLVING SOCIAL RESPONSIBILITY

1. This activity asks you to answer a series of questions regarding your own and your organization's social responsibility:

- Assess what your organization is doing which contributes positively to society, or conversely is damaging the community.
- What are you doing currently to help your community, eg Business in the Community projects?
- What role do you and your team play in that?
- What charitable activities does your organization get involved in?
- What is your role in each of those activities?
- What are you doing to promote involvement in charitable organizations?
- How are you encouraging your team and peers to be more involved in community or charity work?
- Give two examples of how you have helped colleagues who needed help in the last six weeks – what did you do and how did it help?

2. This activity will help if you need a process for finding common ground when it looks as though there is none during a disagreement. The purpose is not to prevent conflict but to manage it so that the team can continue to work effectively together on future changes.

- Ask the teams who have the disagreement to an agreed venue and time.
- Set ground rules with both teams:
  - Each team will take it in turns to have their say.
  - Whoever is speaking should not be interrupted.
  - Everyone will listen calmly and respectfully to what is being said.
  - When the facilitator (you) makes an intervention, everyone else should stop talking.
  - If the teams are unable to reach a solution at the end of the process, tell the group that you will make the decision.
- Ask for a representative from a team to give their perspective of the situation.
- Ask for another person from the same team who may have a different or neutral view on the situation to summarize what was said.

- If different information arises as a result of this do not allow that to be challenged but focus on it as more information.

- Repeat the same process with the other team.

- When both teams have had their say, ask all teams to highlight any points of agreement that they noticed – write them on a flip chart.

- Offer other points of agreement you have noted, eg 'You both agree that it is the customer experience we are trying to improve here.'

- When all agreement points have been logged ask the teams to generate as many creative ways as possible to resolve the situation and write these on a flip chart. Set some ground rules for generation of ideas:
  - No idea is a silly idea.
  - The teams should think of solutions that would take into account both sides of the story.
  - The teams should try to think of a completely different, radical approach to the situation rather than simply trying to fix what is not working at the moment.

- When all ideas have been generated find out if there is one idea all teams are happy to work with and if so help the groups action it.

- If there are no obvious solutions, ask each team to take the ideas away and come up with what their preferred option would be, the benefits for both parties and the end goal and present it to both teams in the morning.

- If neither team is able to do that, select whatever solution you believe would solve the situation and work with both teams to action it.

3. This activity will help if you need to influence someone to do something different for the sake of the team or the change project. It may be that one of your change managers is not implementing things the way that he or she needs to be or he or she is not doing it at all. Giving feedback will be essential during the course of a change project. It can be done in a way that maintains your relationship and without conflict. Follow this six-step process:

- Describe in detail the problem you have observed. Keep your description factual and objective.

- Indicate why it concerns you.

- Ask for reasons that the problem exists and listen openly to the explanation. Listen with empathy. If others become emotional do not interrupt them, offer them encouragement and support.

- Indicate that the situation must change, explain why and ask for ideas for solving the problem. Ask individuals to generate the ideas and do not judge ideas at this stage.

- Discuss each idea and offer your help. Allow time for all ideas to be voiced.

- Agree on specific action to be taken and fix a follow-up date. Ask individuals what support they need from you. Express your confidence in individuals.

25

Gearing up to change – final thoughts

The picture painted throughout this book indicates that there is plenty of scope to follow the change compass and become excellent change managers. Frequently managers are unclear of their distinct contribution and how they add value to the change process. As a result of reading this book, you are now ready to start re-evaluating your contribution, by reassessing honestly what you are doing to manage change, through considering such issues as:

- how much you now know about change;
- your effectiveness in the change process;
- the roles you are fulfilling and the culture you are engendering;
- your value-adding competencies;
- the measures of performance that you and your colleagues are using;
- how you are structured to facilitate change.

COMMON BLOCKS INHIBITING CHANGE

Work on developing excellence in change management must take account of potential blocks to progress. In the book we have talked through many of them. It is worth reiterating some of the most important, based on our experience:

- Whatever the official words of support, senior and middle management in particular can seek to protect old territorial boundaries. It is therefore essential to involve these influential groups in open debate and gain their commitment at the outset.

- Organizational barriers can slow down and inhibit change. Change will suffer through people simply not knowing who to contact, the range of work in which others are involved and poor general communication across groups.

- Despite the growth of e-mail, the Internet and other technologies, there is no substitute for developing strong personal relationships. This is particularly important in truly understanding other people's perspectives.

- Cultural barriers are much harder to overcome than some people expect. But working on common tasks or projects often speeds up the process, if open discussions and review of difficulties are encouraged.

- Parochial, inward thinking is common before many initiatives start. A common perception is: 'I don't need to change'. By seeing the world through such a restricted lens the effect is to narrow down possibilities for innovation and cross-fertilization to improve effectiveness. Do not let this deter you from making long-term change, work at listening to the concerns and dealing with those. Create a positive, can-do environment.

SUCCESS FACTORS SUPPORTING CHANGE

- Be prepared for a long-term investment in change. No 'quick hit' is likely to achieve lasting change.

- Any successful change process is likely to involve an attitude and behaviour shift. To do this successfully, managers will need to touch hearts and deep-seated attitudes as well as rational minds. This requires skilful leadership and a strong vision.

- Visible top management support is a strong factor in sustaining momentum. Having managers spending time giving out recognition awards, holding briefing sessions, putting change on every management meeting agenda is not a 'nice to have' situation, it is a necessity.

- Consider piloting substantial change, targeting key groups initially and those with potential to move into important roles to deliver maximum impact. However, long term this should involve more than just selected groups.

- Follow-up activity is key, since implementation can be a lonely business if the culture is hostile or where workload is high. Mentoring and coaching can be valuable aids.

- The strengthening of networking and two-way communication is vital in overcoming any hurdles and building commitment to a new culture.

- Improvements and change initiatives need to be viewed in the context of a total business strategy, which includes re-assessing organizational structure, business processes, team working, organizational culture and its symbols, reward and promotion structures.

- Involvement of stakeholders, such as customers and employees, in any change process will ensure that they are kept fully in the picture, their ideas incorporated and any potential reservations are taken into account.

- Design initiatives that fit the context in which the organization is operating. Form partnerships with outside specialists where appropriate.

- Check out in advance how the areas undergoing change interface with other parts of the organization and examine related processes. Seek to resolve conflicts of aims, values and interests, which may undermine progress.

- Communicate widely, internally and externally at every stage.

- Manage each of the transition stages of change, expecting people to go through phases of denial, rejection and acceptance before fully taking on board the change message.

- Monitor and evaluate success at regular intervals, using measures agreed at the start.

Below is a final checklist that provides a summary examination of change issues in your organization.

Tick the appropriate column for each of these statements	Yes	No	More work needed
Our change vision is clear.			
Managers are leaders in demonstrating change behaviours.			
We know clearly the profile of change agents.			
We listen to our customers and are quick to respond to them.			

Tick the appropriate column for each of these statements	Yes	No	More work needed
We have reward and recognition processes that value creative, proactive and enthusiastic change.			
We introduce innovations regularly.			
Individual development plans are in place that link personal and organizational goals.			
Development and training is a priority.			
Managers and team leaders support, not stifle learning from change.			
Communications systems are thorough and two-way.			
We regularly seek employees' views and act on the results.			
Our ability to manage change ranks well with: a) our sector; b) best practice in other sectors.			
We encourage employees to expect change, and to be stimulated by this environment.			

CONCLUSION

Make the change compass your own. It would be easy to put change management down to a few simple formulae. However, staying ahead in the competitive race is always more stretching. It is far more than knowing the theory or principles of what should be done. What really makes the difference is the practical application of change management principles day in, day out, on a consistent basis across all aspects of how the organization does business.

There are excellent organizations that model best practice in the way they manage change and this book has given you some examples. Even if you cannot copy their methods exactly, you can learn from their experiences. The path to creating a truly change-oriented organization lies in us examining others' experiences and relating them to our own context. If we share this learning and put energy behind it, our potential can be realized to provide truly exemplary change management.

References

Ansoff, H I (1987) *Corporate Strategy*, Penguin revised edition, London

Baddeley, S and James, K (1987) Owl, fox, donkey or sheep: political skills for managers, *Management Education and Development*, **18** (1), pp 3–19

Belasco, J A and Stayer, R C (1995) *The Flight of the Buffalo*, Little Brown, New York

Bennis W, 'On Becoming a Leader: The Leadership Classic – updated and expanded' (April 2003), Perseus Books Group, Cambridge, MA

Burke W, 'Organisational Change: Theory and Practice' (2002) Sage Publications, Thousand Oaks

Carlson, J R, Carlson, D and Wadsworth, L (2000) The Relationship Between Individual Influence Attempts and Group Agreement, *SAM Advanced Management Journal*, **65** (4), pp 44–51

Cassani, B (2003) *Go: An Airline Adventure*, Time Warner, New York

Dell, M (1999) *Direct from Dell: Strategies that revolutionized an industry*, Harper Business, New York

Dervitsiotis, K N (1998) The challenge of managing organizational change: Exploring the relationship of re-engineering, developing learning organizations and total quality management, *Total Quality Management*, **9**, (1) p 109 (14)

Frankl, V (1984) *Man's Search for Meaning*, Simon and Schuster, New York

French, J R P and Raven, B (1968) The Bases of Social Power, in *Group Dynamics*, eds D Cartwright and A Zander, pp 150–167, Harper and Row, New York

Goleman, D (1995) *Emotional Intelligence*, Bantam Books, New York

Handy, C (1997) The Search for Meaning: A Conversation with Charles Handy, *Leader to Leader*, **5**, Summer

Handy, C _et al_ (1999) _Inside Organizations_, Penguin Business, London

Heskett, J L and Sasser, W E and Schlesinger, L A (1997) The Service Profit Chain, The Free Press, Simon & Schuster Inc., New York

Higgs, M and Rowland, D (2002) Does it need emotional intelligence to lead change? _Journal of General Management_, **27** (3) Spring

Johnson, G and Scholes, J (1993) _Exploring Corporate Strategy Text and cases_, 3rd edn, Prentice Hall, Hemel Hempstead

Kelly, M (2003) _The Divine Right of Capital_, Bennett-Koehler, San Francisco

Kubler-Ross, E (1975) _Death the final stage of growth_, Prentice Hall, New York

Lewin, K (1951) _Field Theory in Social Sciences_, Harper Collins, New York

Maurer, R (1997) Transforming resistance (managing organizational change), _HR Focus_, 74 (10), p 9 (2)

Maslow, A H (1954) _Motivation and Personality_, Harper & Row, New York

Mayer, J D and Salovey, P (1997) 'What is Emotional Intelligence?' in P Salovey and D Sluyter (eds), 'Emotional Development and Emotional Intelligence: Implications for Educators', pp 3–31 BasicBooks, New York

McLaughlin, C (1994) _Spirituality Politics: Changing the world from the inside out_, Ballantine, Washington

McLaughlin, C and Davidson, G (2002) _Spiritual Approaches to Energising your Company_, The Center for Visionary Leadership, Washington

Pickard, J (2002) 'Top Gear', _People Management_, 18 April

Porter, M E (1985) 'Competitive Advantage: Creating & Sustaining Superior Performance', The Free Press, Simon & Schuster Inc., New York

Robbins, S P (2001) _Organizational Behavior_, 7th edn, Prentice Hall, New Jersey

Ruderman, M, Hannum, K and Brittan Leslie, J (2003) Emotional intelligence and career derailment, _Competency and Emotional Intelligence Journal_, **10** (3) Spring

Schein, E H (1996) _Organizational Culture and Leadership_, 2nd edn, Jossey-Bass, New York

Senge, P (1994) _The Fifth Discipline Fieldbook_, Nicholas Brearley, London

Senge, P (2001) _Leadership in the World of the Living_, http:www.gwsae.org/ThoughtLeaders/SengeLeadership.htm (retrieved 18 March 2003)

Spitzer, D R (1995) _Supermotivation_, Anacom, New York

Tannenbaum, R and Schmidt, W H (1973) How to Choose a Leadership Pattern, _Harvard Business Review_, May-June

Venschoov, C, Prof (2003) _Management Consultancy_, Sept-Oct

Whitmore, J (1997) _Need, Greed or Freedom_, Element Books, Dorset

Wustemann, L (2001) Emotional Intelligence and the bottom line, _Competency and Emotional Intelligence Journal_, **9** (2) Winter 2001–2

Further reading

BQ

Collins, J (2001) *Good to Great*, Random House, London
Hammer, M and Champy, J (2001) *Re-engineering the Corporation: Manifesto for business revolution*, paperback edn, Harper Business, London
Kotter, J (2002) *The Heart of Change*, Harvard Business School, Boston, MA
Obolensky, N (1994) *Business Re-engineering*, Kogan Page, London
Olivier, R (2001) *Inspirational Leadership*, The Industrial Society, London
Reichheld, F (1996) *The Loyalty Effect*, Harvard Business School, Boston, MA
Reichheld, F (2001) *Loyalty Rules*, Harvard Business School, Boston, MA
Thompson, J (2001) *Strategic Management*, Thomson Learning, London

SQ

Dilts, R (1994) *Strategies of Genius*, Meta Publications, Capitola CA
Handy, C (1998) *The Hungry Spirit*, Arrow, London
McLaughlin, C and Davidson, G (1998) 'Spiritual Approaches to Energising Your Company' audiotape, The Centre for Visionary Leadership, Washington DC
Zohar, D and Marshall, I (2000) *SQ The Ultimate Intelligence*, Bloomsbury Publishing, New York

PQ

Butcher, D and Clarke, M (2001) _Smart Management_, Palgrave, Basingstoke

Cava, R (1990) _Dealing with Difficult People_, Piatkus Books, London

Crawely, J (1992) _Constructive Conflict Management_, Nicholas Brearley, London

Patching, K, Chatham, R (2000) _Corporate Politics for IT Managers_, Butterworth Heinmann, Oxford

Robinson, C (1990) _Winning at Business Negotiations_, Kogan Page, London

Steele, P, Murphy, J and Russill, R (1989) _It's a Deal_, McGraw-Hill, Maidenhead

Ury, W (1992) _Getting Past No_, Randon House Business Books, London

EQ

Cooper, R and Sawaf, A (2000) _Executive EQ_, Texere, London

Covey, S (1999) _Seven Habits of Highly Successful People_, Simon and Schuster, New York

Goleman, D (1998) _Working with Emotional Intelligence_, Bloomsbury, London

Knight, S (1995) _NLP at Work_, Nicholas Brearley, London

Orme, G (2001) _Emotionally Intelligent Living_, Crown House Publishing, Bancyfelin

Stein, S J and Book, H E (2003) _The EQ Edge_, Multi-Health Systems Inc., Toronto

Sterrett, E A (2000) _Emotional Intelligence_, HRD Press, Amherst

Index

Page references in *italics* indicate figures, tables or activities

Also available from Kogan Page:

Customer Care Excellence
How to Create an Effective Customer Focus
4th Edition
Sarah Cook

"…addresses the issue of customer care and offers useful advice on maintaining loyalty within an ever more sophisticated and demanding customer base. …informative and useful for anybody involved in customer relations."
Business Age

Today's consumers are sophisticated, well informed and have high expectations of the services they want to receive. They want greater choice, speed of service, convenience and will not be 'sold to' or manipulated. Companies that do not face up to these changes will lose market share.

The fourth edition of *Customer Care Excellence* recognizes these trends and demonstrates in a clear, practical way how to develop and sustain a customer-service focus. The book places a great emphasis on the strategic aspects of customer care – gaining commitment, listening to customers, developing a customers-care ethos and motivating employees to deliver excellent service – in ensuring successful results.

The above title is available from all good bookshops. To obtain further information, please contact the publisher at the address below:

Kogan Page
120 Pentonville Road
London N1 9JN
Tel: 020 7278 0433
Fax: 020 7837 6348
www.kogan-page.co.uk

Also available from Kogan Page:

Making Sense of Change Management
A Complete Guide to the Models, Tools & Techniques of Organizational Change
Esther Cameron & Mike Green

"This impressive book on change is an essential read for any professional manager who is serious about getting to grips with the important issues of making change happen."
Dr Jeff Watkins, MSc Course Director, University of Bristol

"There has long been a need for a readable, practical but theoretically underpinned book on change which recognizes a multiplicity of perspectives. I thoroughly recommend it."
Professor Colin Carnall, Associate Dean, Executive Programme, Warwick Business School, University of Warwick

"This book is a great resource for managers thrown into the midst of change, who need to gain understanding of what happens when you try to make significant changes in a business, and how best to manage people through it."
Andy Newall, Organizational Effectiveness Director, Allied Domecq plc

Making Sense of Change Management is about making change easier. It is aimed at anyone who wants to understand why change happens, how it happens and what needs to be done to make change a welcome rather than a dreaded concept. However, this book is not a 'one size fits all' simplistic panacea to all change, whatever the circumstances. Instead it offers considered insights into the many frameworks, models and ways of approaching change and helps the reader to apply the right approach to each unique situation.

The above title is available from all good bookshops. To obtain further information, please contact the publisher at the address below:

Kogan Page
120 Pentonville Road
London N1 9JN
Tel: 020 7278 0433
Fax: 020 7837 6348
www.kogan-page.co.uk